Defying the Odds

Becoming the Best Possible You...

No Matter the Cost

10.14.19

James Merrifield

BEYOND

New York | Los Angeles | London | Sydney

10 9 8 7 6 5 4 3 2 1

Library of Congress: 2018944321

Second Edition 978-1-947256-73-6

Hard back 978-1-947256-50-7

ebook 978-1-947256-51-4

Spanish perfect bound 978-1-947256-52-1

Table of Contents

Preface

I have faced many trials and tribulations in my life. There were many struggles and more obstacles than I can remember. But one thing is for sure, and that is that I never gave up on my dreams. The sole purpose of this book is to motivate, inspire, and encourage others to be their absolute best, no matter what life may throw in their direction. By sharing my life experiences with others, I hope to help people make the world a better place for everyone.

I have always felt as if my life was like a movie, and now it is time that I share it with all of you. There are many inspirational life stories out there for one to read, but my story is very unique. Some of these real-life events are breath-taking and recounted with no filters. I want my audience to experience my story in all its fullness. This is a story that I am dedicating to those of us who didn't have it so easy in life. I'm here to represent for the under dogs and for the individuals that no one expected to succeed, and for those who had to work day and night to reverse a vicious cycle so that their families could have the life that they always dreamed of. This is for you.

If you believe that you can achieve, then you are already there. You just don't know it yet. The Law of Attraction states that what you think about you will become. All my life, I always knew that I was different. I always felt different. I did not fit in. I was destined for greatness and, when I found that my true calling was to help others, it was then that my real work began. This is my life; this is my story. I hope that you will take something good from this book and go out there and make a difference in this world.

Special Thanks

I would like to give the highest praise and thanks to Jesus Christ, who has had my back since day one. In my darkest moments, He was the only one who was there for me to pull me through the tough times. Each day, just before the sun comes up, I am sure to give thanks for all of my blessings. Thank You, Lord, for the cloud you made for me. I know You put it there for all of us to see.

Growing up I did not have a father like the one that I became for my children, but I had a woman's love that carried me through this life. Thank you, Mom, for loving me unconditionally, and for believing in me for all of these years.

My three children Ashley, Cody, and James are my biggest motivation to NEVER give up on my goals and, most importantly, myself. I strived to reach EXCELLENCE in my parenting, and I was determined to NEVER let them down or make them go without anything. I have dedicated my life to my kids. I will forever be their protector and provide them with knowledge and wisdom. I love them with all of my heart.

Last but not least, I want to thank my beautiful wife, Veronica Rosales Merrifield. For the last eleven years Veronica has been an incredible support to this family. She is the nicest, most kind- hearted, and loving person in the world and I am truly blessed to be married to her. Thank you, My Love, for saving me. I don't know where I would be or what I would do without you. You make this family complete, and I am forever grateful for you.

Chapter 1: Where It All Began

It was a warm summer night in Los Angeles County, California. The year was 1985 and I was about six years old. My dad and I had just been dropped off at the bus stop on Atlantic Boulevard in Alhambra, California and we were en route to visit my grandmother.

That day we had been hanging out at my Great-Uncle Jimmy's apartment in the East Los Angeles Projects. My dad and his uncle had killed a couple of cases of Budweiser and a bottle of Thunder Bird. They had also smoked that "sherm stick," better known to most as PCP. At the end of the day, my dad was exhausted from partying so hard. The look in his eye was more like the party is coming to an end. I had seen him this way many times throughout my young life. In fact, he was so exhausted that we had to stop about a half mile from my grandma's house because he was about to pass out in the Northrup Elementary school yard. He had partied his ass off that day, and he just couldn't hang anymore.

That day I remember my dad staring down at the concrete with lost eyes. Then he broke down and began to cry. This was not some touching Hollywood-style breakdown; it was more like long, wailing, pain-filled howls, like a wolf baying at the moon. He was intoxicated to the point that he passed out and then urinated all over himself. It was now about 11 p.m., and that night we slept on the lunch tables just outside of Northrup Elementary School on a busy street on Atlantic Boulevard, Whether I liked it or not.

Forty years later I can still hear that tormented wail if it happened just yesterday. No matter what I went through as a child, no matter what I was exposed to, my dad was my hero. He was everything to me just as I am to my three children. As a child, it broke my heart to hear him cry like that. As an adult, I now understand why he did.

I believe that my dad wanted his family back. But it was too late. The damage was done. He fucked up one time too many and now it was over. Please make a mental note that I do believe in the concept of forgiveness, but at the same time I also believe in the concept of "it's too late," "enough is enough," and "we are finished." The bottom line is that you can't go on forever hurting those in your inner circle. Sad to say, much of the time, those who take the biggest advantage of you will be those who are closest to you. Those who hurt you the most are last people you would have thought would commit such atrocity.

When he awoke at about 3 a.m., I was so happy because I knew that Grandma's house wasn't too far away. I could have a roof over my head, sleep on a soft sofa and feel safe. Finally, I could just relax.

Trust me that night was fucked up.

But It was during that walk home that I learned another valuable life lesson and this would be one of many lessons that I would learn from my dad. The lesson was to never put my children in that same predicament. The lesson was to never put myself in that type of situation. The lesson was to never let something like alcohol or drugs dictate my life to the point of self-destruction. I have lived my entire life learning from the mistakes of others. This was just one of the first of many life lessons.

Learning from other peoples' mistakes is one of the biggest contributors to my success. When I became an adult, I was more prepared to survive and ready to do battle with life's challenges more than most people are due to all the shit that I was exposed to growing up. When you learn to live life in survival mode you learn to think and react real fast. I've always felt as if my life was like a movie with many scenes in the areas of hardship, heart break, life challenges, both victory, and defeat. But most important there are many areas in my life where I was able to learn and grow so that now I can share it with the world and help others grow.

Chapter 2: Life in the 80's

In the 1980s, inner city Los Angeles, California was a great place to be. You could witness a murder and see the dead bodies get chalked up on the streets. Families gathered on the sidewalks to see the body hauled away. The sidewalks were packed with innocent by-standers watching the real life novella take place. The very next day, that body chalk outline in the middle of the street became "home plate" as we played baseball all day long in the streets with a bat and a tennis ball. Back in the day we played until the street lights came on or until your mom told you to get inside.

Summer time in L.A. was the best! That was because all of our cousins, aunts, uncles, parents, and grandparents would get together at my Tia Corrine and Uncle Louie's house. Their house on 3rd and Hicks St. in the heart of East LA was the base for my family. There are many golden memories that took place in their home. But most important it was a place of love and togetherness. In the streets of East Los Angeles raspada and ice cream trucks rolled down the streets and blaired music on the loud speaker for all to hear, like a car club on parade. These trucks were battling it out for business day in and day out.

The Cholos and the Cholas ran those streets in a fashion much more different than in today's world. Dudes either had slicked back hair or a buzz cut and the girls wore their hair feathered with a ton of Aqua Net hair spray to keep their bangs in place. Both guys and the girls wore 501 Levi's with extra starch on those creases, and fresh white t-shirt with a Pendleton to match. That was the look of the hood.

No matter what was going on in that neck of the woods, kids were loved beyond belief and were always made to feel very special. We were always treated with kindness and much more love than what many kids experience today. Most importantly, we all loved each other.

Sure there was violence just as there would be in any inner city area. But this was life. This is what I was exposed to growing up in my early years.

Today the world is filled with more hate than ever. Kids are taking assault rifles to schools and opening fire on innocent people. When we turn to blame guns for the tragedy it is my belief that hate is the root cause for these acts of terror. Hate in its full bloom leads to death and destruction. Most importantly, we all loved each other.

Growing up, I lived in the Pico Rivera projects, better known as the Rivera Villa. Pico Rivera is about 10 miles east of East Los Angeles. The Rivera Villa housing community is no longer around because it was deemed as unsafe and demolished around twenty years ago. For those who are able to say that they played some part in Rivera Villas history, my hat goes off to you. Everything from sex to drugs to murder to rape to overdoses took place in that compound. It was a pimper's paradise.

In the Summer time the swimming pool area went off! In the hood people love to play funk music and oldies very loud. You could hear the bass from the speakers as you pulled in to the complex, as the center of the building looked like the hood version of the Roman Coliseum. People would show up to the building to visit their friends, hang out, buy drugs, and party hard.

Imagine that.

Chapter 3: Casa Blanca

Early in 1983, we had had to leave LA for a few years. I was five years old at the time. We relocated to Riverside for about two years because one of my dad's gang affiliates ended up killing one of my mom's affiliates in The Rivera Villa's. They said that it was an accident and that they were just trying to teach someone a lesson. Yeah, right. No body dies from a gunshot wound in Pico Rivera accidentally. But, somehow somebody snitched that my dad was involved, so we needed to get out of town for a while.

We left Pico Rivera and went to live about 60 miles east in Riverside California. But let me tell you that Riverside was no joke either. In fact, there is a little hell on earth located in Riverside called The Casa Blanca. This gang infested neighborhood was started back in the 1960's and can be traced back to a bar fight between two families, The Ahumada's and the Lozano's. These two families ignited a war on the streets that would not cease until all of the men on both sides were a total genocide.

My cousins living in Riverside were from the gang called Casa Blanca. Casa Blanca is composed of several sub-click gangs. To me it was, and still to this day is one of the scariest neighborhoods I have ever seen. There is only one way into that neighborhood and one way out.

At the age of 5 years old I was sent to pre-school dead center of the heart of Casa Blanca.

My mom, for whatever reason, just could not stay away from that gang banger lifestyle. She used to leave me with my uncles at night when she went out with her cousins. I knew that my older cousins were heavily involved in the Casa Blanca gang activity. When my mom would leave for the night I used to pray to God that He would bring my mom home safe because I knew what went on after dark in the Casa Blanca. There were real killers on the loose in that part of town and at night is when the shit went down.

My Aunt Peachie and Uncle Johnny lived in Casa Blanca with their five children Diana, Peter, Anthony, Gabriel, and John Jr. All of them were gang affiliated in one way or another.

As a youth I spent a lot of time with my younger cousins—John Jr. aka John John and Gilbert, who was the youngest of their children. There were several bullet holes all over the walls and on the mirrors of Aunt Peachie and Uncle Johnny's house. When we spent the night as kids, Aunt Peachie made us sleep on the floor. That's how bad it was. Bullets were flying every night in Casa Blanca. They even shot down a police helicopter in that neighborhood! Casa Blanca in the 1980s was the real deal and they were not backing down to anyone.

Looking back I still get an eerie feeling as I knew that I didn't want to be there.

One day my mom came home real late in the night and I overheard hear her talking to someone on the phone. She was telling them about how she was hanging out at the park in Casa Blanca when rival gang members came through and did a drive bye on her and our cousins. They shot at my mom and ended up hitting her car. I remember going outside the next day and seeing the bullet holes in my mom's car. Thank God she wasn't killed that night. I fuckin hated when she would take off at night, because that meant that my nights as a kid were filled with thoughts of the worst as one can only imagine what happens in a place of danger.

We stayed in Riverside for about two years. These were the years that I have the most memories of my parents being together. My mom and dad were my life. I just wanted them to get along so that we could live together in peace. My uncles Marty, David, and Greg lived with us too, along with my Grandpa Tony. My Grandpa Tony was literally the glue that held our family together. It is my belief that I got my hard work ethic from him as he provided the needs for his entire family until the day of his death.

We lived in Riverside for a few years in the early 1980s. I have many memories there, some good and some bad. I learned how to ride a bike and hit a baseball. My dad and I would lace up our boots as used to hike up and down the mountain at Arlington and the 91 freeway with our dogs. MTV started a music revolution that would create the soundtrack of my life. To this day whenever I hear the song "Back on the chain gang" by the Pretenders it takes my back to that era. As the song states "I found a picture of you, those were the happiest days of my life." YES!! For me the 1980's were the golden years. The song clearly reminds me of my youth with my parents. Some of the best days of my young life took place there in Riverside.

As a kid, no matter what went on, all I knew was that my mom and dad were still together and we were a family. All I ever wanted in life was for us to be a family. But it just could not happen as my dad was an extremely violent drunk and would beat my mom down as if she were a man. I hated to see that happen. He used to beat me down too. Sometimes he would just look at me and I would start to cry because I knew that I was going to get my ass kicked. Still, my parents were my only security blanket and I just wished that they could work it out, but they didn't and in 1985, my parents decided to not be together anymore.

Fast forward years later, in 1993, my sophomore year in high school, cousin Gilbert would be murdered in Casa

Blanca. Both he and his girlfriend's father were lit up from head to toe with an uzi sub machine gun.

It was at a celebration of Gilbert's girlfriend's 17th birthday party and some rival gang members showed up uninvited. The girl's father asked them to leave and they left, only to drive around the back alley, stand up on the hoods of their cars so that they could see over the wall, and open fire on everyone in the back yard. It was a slaughter.

Lying in that box, my cousin Gilbert looked so young, like when we were kids, except he had a small goat tee on his baby face along with a few scars. Looking at him, I couldn't help but remember when we were kids eating bananas, pretending to be monkeys, and hanging upside down in the trees of the front yard in Casa Blanca. He was now dead at just 16 years old.

All of Gilberts friends from his gang were present at the funeral. I could still see their cold stares as they were standing around the corner of the building with their backs turned against the wall in wait of a possible ambush. They do that kind of shit at a gang related funeral. It's a perfect opportunity for your enemies to catch you and your entire team slipping in the same place, and they will take you out.

Those boys were serious a fuck as they believed that vengeance belonged to them.

14

When someone dies in my family we eat pan dulce, (Mexican Sweet Bread) drink coffee, and hot chocolate on the night of the wake. The day after we bury you, we eat menudo with bollilos (Mexican style baked roll) and drink alcohol VERY heavily.

On the day of the burial we went to Aunt Peachies for the farewell get together. I walked in the house and instantaneously remembered everything in that house just as I did as a kid.

The bullet holes in the mirrors and walls and sleeping on the ground at night.

As I walked by my Aunt Peachie's room, I heard the saddest cry I had ever heard in all of my life. It was a cry of deep pain and great sadness. The weeping was very soft and calm. I helplessly stood there and watched her lying face down on her bed. I took one last look at the bullet hole riddled mirrors and walls and then told myself that, after today, I would not be coming back to Casa Blanca ever again.

Today, all my male cousins from the Casa Blanca area, except for one, took a bullet in the head and are no longer alive.

As I now stand at the age of 40 years old the question that I ask myself is "Why didn't my aunt Peach and Uncle John sell the house and just move away?" Why on earth would you stay in a place where you knew that extreme gang violence would someday rob you of your family? I don't believe that I will ever figure that out. I know enough to know that my family's safety means everything to me and if I had to up and leave to preserve their lives, I wouldn't have to think twice about it.

****

Chapter 4: Christmas Day 1986

My mom and dad parted ways in 1985. She had had enough of getting her ass kicked. I still remember the day that my dad packed his stuff and announced that he was leaving. My mom sarcastically said that my dad was leaving because he didn't love us anymore and of course a fight immediately broke out. She actually got away before he could strike her. I was sad to see this break up happen but at the same time I was tired of the violence.

My dad went back to live in Alhambra with my Grandma Josie. The days of Riverside had come to an end for all of us as me and my mom migrated back to Pico Rivera.

When I went to spend time with my dad in Alhambra he used to take me to work with him. We would take the bus to the big construction sites. I would spend the day with him and Grandpa Tony working from sun up, to sun down. My grandfather loved my dad as if he were his own son. Even after my parents parted ways, my grandfather looked after my dad until the day he died. Clearly Dad was his right-hand man on those construction sights. Grandpa Tony was a mentor to my father. He showed him the construction trade. He taught him how to work hard for his money.

I remember one year in particular, in 1986. I got to spend Christmas with my dad and his girlfriend. Though I don't think that my mom was too excited about me not being with her for the holiday, I was really excited to be with him. I missed my dad and not being able to see him daily was taking a toll on me. Both of my parents had already started to get involved with other people. My mom was already seeing Huero and My Dad ended up with a blond girl named Heather.

A few months before Christmas my dad asked in advance what presents I wanted, so I already knew that I was getting. I only wanted two things that year; a remote control car and a plush Alf doll that talked. I wasn't very hard to please.

Dad appeared to be making big strides to improve his life. I was really proud of him. He seemed to be maturing and growing in to a responsible human being. He went out and bought two matching Nissan Trucks for his lady and himself. He also got himself a nice little two-bedroom apartment in Alhambra. I was just happy to be with him. No matter what, I loved this man with all my heart. Back then, he meant the world to me. But no matter how good he seemed to be doing, he was still very undisciplined in his mind and in his actions.

Christmas Day came, and we already opened our gifts. I was so excited to have a stuffed talking ALF toy and a brand-new remote controlled car!! I went outside and raced it up and down the apartment complex until the batteries died!! That Christmas was memorable in a lot of ways for me, but one thing in particular makes it really stand out. To make a long story short, on that Christmas Day, my dad went to jail for assault and battery.

His girlfriend had a daughter who was about three years younger than me. Heather already had her kid trained to call my dad "Dad." I think my dad could tell that I wasn't too thrilled about it. I became very jealous and was not too fond of her doing that. My dad saw that his girlfriend was allowing her kid to get under my skin and asked Heather a few times to stop it. She wasn't taking him very seriously and, out of nowhere, he snapped.

I had seen my dad do this many times to my mom, but on this Christmas day I saw him do it to his girlfriend and to a whole new level like I never saw before. I watched my dad mount Heather like a UFC fighter and beat her into submission.

When he was finished, he let her up and kicked her ass all the way out the front door. When she tried to leave, he snatched her up by her hair and told her to "get the fuck inside and put some shoes on."

I knew she wasn't going to let him get away with that and, within minutes, the police were knocking at the door. My dad was ultra-calm when the police asked him if he was Leo Merrifield and if he was the one who beat up his girlfriend. He said in the calmest voice, "Yes." He wasn't scared of the police nor did he act out of line or attempt to resist them. It was almost as if he just expected to go to jail. It was as if he just knew that he had it coming to him.

In my mind I can still see this take place like if it were yesterday. I cried as the police took him away. His girlfriend immediately threw me in the truck and dumped me off at my Grandma Josie's apartment. On the way there she said that she was sorry that that happened and made it a point to let me know that she wasn't a punching bag.

I was really sad that this had happened. Especially because it took place on Christmas Day. Like I said before, this wasn't my first rodeo, just as it was not my dads. My frustration came from the fact that we just couldn't get it right! We just could not live a normal life! But then again...does a normal life even exist? Bottom line...I just always felt like such a loser. My life structure was fucked up and I knew it. All I knew was that someday when it was my turn to be a father, I would never allow history to repeat itself!! To this very day, I absolutely hate it when I hear about men beating women. It is my belief that a woman can no longer be a woman of self and inner beauty after her man beats her down. Her beautiful essence is gone. Fear will set in to her mind and plague her for all eternity. The memory of such acts is a life sentence that will never go away.

My mother once told my ex-wife that my dad would call her from the bar after he had been out partying with his friends all night to say that he would be coming home soon. She said that, when she heard the tone in his voice, she knew that he was drunk and she would begin to shake in fear. I know that feeling.

Sometimes he would just look at me, and I would start to cry because I knew what was coming. I knew what that ass whopping felt like. I hated that shit.

Chapter 5: The Welfare Office

After the Christmas episode at Dad's, I went back home with my mom. By that time, we were living back in Pico Rivera. One day, when I was about eight years old, Mom took me with her to the welfare office. She was there to ask for money and some food stamps. It appeared that mom hit rock bottom and she needed some help. I will never forget the day because that trip to the welfare office changed my life forever.

A female social worker came into the room. She looked at my mom and asked, "What are you here for today?" My mom began to cry. She was so in defeat. To this day I can still hear her voice in my mind as she replied, "I don't have any money." As she cried, the social worker told her it that was going to be okay and that she was there to help her. At that point, I told myself in my mind, "Fuck that!"

Right there, I made a promise to myself that I would never allow myself to be in a position like that! I would work my ass off so that my kids would have whatever they might need! I would do whatever it took to not be broke! Literally!

However, please make a mental note that I do support the welfare system. And we can debate all day and night about welfare abuse and people taking advantage of the system. Look at foreign countries in South America and In the Middle East parts of the world. With no welfare system in place that would be us right here in the United States of America. Imagine that. We have a lot to be grateful for.

That day at the welfare office gave me a scar on my heart the size of the Grand Canyon. No doubt we would have starved if it weren't for the government cheese, and I am very grateful for the food. My point is that, at eight years old, I was already raising the standard for what I wanted for my life and for my future family. That day I told myself that, no matter what, I would man up and do whatever it took to feed my family. Whatever it took.

1986 rolled around and I began to spend a lot more time with my Grandfather Tony. He was my dude. My Love. No one could ever take this man's place. Whatever I needed, he provided, and he was the bridge between my mom and my dad. He was very instrumental in keeping us all together. He was the reason that, for the time being, I was still able to see my dad on a regular basis. Grandpa Tony came and picked me up EVERY weekend without fail. I was so excited when the school bell rang on Friday because I knew in a few hours Grandpa was coming to pick me up. It felt like he came just to see me, and I loved him for that. People might forget about you in one way or another, but they will always remember the way you made them feel and that man made me feel loved. I always felt loved in his presence.

On Fridays my best memories of this man were heading to the liquor store at about 6pm. He always bought me whatever little cheap ghetto toy that I wanted, as he would also purchase a pack of cigarettes, two tall cans of beer, and a fifth of Long Island ice tea. He downed the entire bottle of Long Island on the way out of the parking lot and then threw the bottle out the window. And then with the quickness he began to chase it down with a beer. The music was blasting rock n roll music and the tires were screeching as the light turned green. It was Friday and the party was just getting started.

Chapter 6: Grandpa Tony Dies

Following on the heels of the welfare office episode, the summer of 1986 came quickly, and I was very excited that school was officially over for the year. Little did I know that this day also would change my life forever.

My mom showed up to school early that day. She looked lost and very pale. As we got in the truck and my mom told me that my Grandpa Tony was dead.

My heart just sank.

He was my biggest supporter. The man had never let me down. Not once! And now he was gone.

 He was the bridge connection between my parents and had helped keep my dad in my life. By far, he was one of my absolute most favorite human beings. I must admit that when I was a kid, he was so crazy that he used to scare the crap out of me, but once you got to know him, he was the kindest, funniest, most generous, and most loving person that you were ever going to meet. He had so much love in his heart. He showed us through his own actions that family comes first.   Through his own generosity he would literally take the shirt off of his back for a cold homeless man in the streets, if he had asked him to do so. He would take care the needs of ANY ONE of his family members if they had asked him to do so. He simply had a pure unconditional love for mankind, and that makes me very proud to say that I knew him and was a part of his life.

The night before, he had been out with one of his nephews. Like a "rolling stone," my Grandpa had always loved to party. He had the cash and wasn't afraid to flaunt it. So when it came time to have fun he always went all out.

On the night of his death both he and his nephew Joey were posted up in a ghetto hotel somewhere in L.A. with some hookers and some cocaine. That night they partied hard like rock stars.

Well, that night my grandpa did a little too much of everything. He ended passing out and choking on his own vomit. By the time his nephew found him, it was already too late. His death hit us all hard. It really fucked things up for all my uncles and my aunt, but especially my mom. My mom loved her dad with all of her heart and soul. She was never the same after his death. To this day, she still talks about all the good things that he taught her and about how much she misses him.

Grandpa's death affected my dad, too. My dad had been very close to my grandpa. My grandfather had always treated my dad as a son and had shown him the trade of construction, he showed him by example how to take care of his family, and most important, he showed him love. Both of them were extremely close to one another. But now, they were no longer a team. My grandpa was dead.

Looking back in history just before I was born, my dad had an older brother named George. When they were growing up they resided in East L.A. off the 60 fwy in a neighborhood known as Little Valley. My dad idolized his big brother. When you grow up in the hood all of the boys want to be tough guys and I was told that my uncle George was a bad ass dude who already had a big reputation for claiming the neighborhood and beating people down. But at the age of twenty-one years old George had already developed a very bad habit that would not allow him to see twenty-two years of age.

At twenty-one years of age George drank himself to death.

My mom always said that after George passed away that my dad was never the same.

My dad idolized his big brother and sought to follow him in all of his ways. My dad did all of the same things that George did so that he would be accepted by his big brother. Like younger brothers do my dad just wanted to be like big brother. And he did it so much that he developed all of George's bad habits.

Looking back on the day of that funeral as my dad stared blindly at the concrete lost in thought, I believe that my dad's thoughts were that for the second time in his life he had once again lost his best friend. (Again)

Imagine that. Within a span of just ten short years, two of the most important people that were in your life are now completely gone, forever.

On top of all of this happening my parents did not let me attend Grandpa Tony's funeral, which I thought was pretty fucked up. That day of the funeral I remember sitting in the back yard thinking to myself "What the fuck am I doing here?!" "I should be at the funeral with my family saying goodbye to my grandpa!" My grandpa was a big part of my world, and I didn't even get to say a proper farewell. It really bothered me that I didn't get to say good bye. I desperately wanted to go to his grave site just so that I could tell him that I loved him and that someday I was going to make him very proud of me.

I was just a kid! A kid who needed to be loved! A kid who needed someone solid in his life for security and stability! Someone who would take away my worries and my pains and help me to feel good about myself!

Now grandpa was gone.

Once I was old enough to drive, I immediately made it a point to go visit his grave site at the Resurrection

Cemetery in Rosemead, California. I've been there on several occasions now.

At his grave site I would pop open an expensive bottle of red wine and light up a good imported cigar. I was so happy to talk to him. I would always update him with what was going on in my life and with the rest of the family. Before I left I would tell him that I know that he would have been so proud of me and my kids. I'd tell him how awesome the kids are and how we are doing. I'd tell him about all of the cool things that we would do with our kids and about all of their accomplishments. To this day, I really miss him and wonder what my life would have been like had he not left so soon. My grandpa left this earth at forty-seven years old. I cant help but to wonder would I have gone the same route in life? Or where would I be today had my grandpa lived long enough to see us grow up?

I guess I will never know.

On the day of the funeral, everyone came back to my Uncle's house for beers and menudo.

I watched my dad sit on the porch with a 1.5 liter bottle of red wine. My dad was notorious for drinking until he passed out or drinking until he got violent and started fighting with someone, but that day was a day for the records. As he sat there on the porch drinking his wine, he just stared at the floor. He didn't talk. He didn't engage with anyone. He did tell me, however, that he wanted to kill my cousin for what he had done to my grandpa. For years everyone blamed my cousin for my grandfather's death, but the truth is that **we are where we are in life because we choose to be there.** We can't really blame other people for our choices. No one forces you to do anything. If you play the game, that means that someday you'll pay, and that's exactly what happened. My grandfather paid with his life.

My dad had lost the man who took him in like a son. He was so heartbroken that day. That day was the beginning of the end for many of us. It seemed as if our great big huge family was now shrinking in numbers. Grandpa Tony kept his entire family very close for all of these years. It was now appearing that some parts of the family both close and apart were now beginning to separate and disengage with one another. It was the beginning of more hardships and heart breaks for my family.

Chapter 7: Costa Mesa

About a year later after Grandpa Tony died, we moved to Costa Mesa. Talk about culture shock. Moving from Pico Rivera to Costa Mesa was no easy transition.

I had never physically seen in person blonde hair with blue eyes in all of my life except on episodes of TJ Hooker. The demographic was way different from L.A. and Riverside. Way different.

By then, my mom was already pregnant with my sister and, of course, brought my low life step-dad with us to the OC. So much for a fresh start, right? The saying is very true that you can take the boys (and the girls) out of the hood, but you can't take the hood out of them.

He came from a long line of real killers and convicts. He and his brothers were from a gang called El Monte Flores which is located in the city of El Monte California.

Back in the 1970s The Flores Gang was one of the most well organized and most feared gangs in Los Angeles County. They held real business like meetings and used their drug profits to purchase weapons and keep their people inside of prison well taken care of. They were also one of the first gangs to be tied in to the Mexican Mafia.

I just want to throw it out there that the year before we came to CM, my step-dad stole our Christmas presents and clucked them for his dope. Then he made up some bullshit story about someone breaking in the house and stealing all of them. What a piece of shit, right? Yeah, I remember seeing this dude fresh off shooting up, standing there staring into space like he was John Glenn looking at the moon for the first time. What a sight for a kid to see right? I was never a fan of this man, but my mother was so excited about him. She told me that he did not drink or smoke. Basically, what she was saying was that he didn't do all the things that my dad used to do. She just conveniently left out the part where he was a heroin addict and was always in and out of jail.

This is the kind of behavior that you should NEVER expose your kids or your loved ones to! It will create a memory that they will never be able to forget and even worse…they may just follow in their footsteps. Think about it. The most precious thing in your life—your wife or children—shooting up heroin. How does that visual make you feel? The bottom line is that, in the long run, that person is going to end up in one of two places. Either dead or in prison. There is no grey area on this subject. In today's world heroin has made a major comeback. It's like injecting poison in to your veins is the fun thing to do.

Parents and people of leadership we have got to stand together to eliminate the need for our people to follow in these footsteps. It is not ok for us to watch our loved ones destroy themselves. Once the habit of heroin abuse is formed, not very many people are strong enough to break free from their addiction.

Chapter 8: The Day Huero Stole the Rent Money

So, my step-father was a heroin addict, a thief, and a selfish bastard, which is why I came to despise those individuals so much. They will steal anything from anyone and not even think twice about it. He used to steal my money from my sock drawer for his fix. He stole my mom's wedding ring and pawned it for dope. He even took my brothers' and sister's milk money and ran to the dope man's house with it.

One day he stole our rent money....

He was so sneaky about it. He snatched up the rent money from where my mom hid it in the vacuum, and immediately ran off to the dope man's house in Santa Ana.

This episode was like a movie! My mom woke up from her nap and said, "Where is he?!" I said, "I don't know?" She said, "Get in the truck now!" (It was game on!) It's like she just knew his exact plan! She sped off up the street and drove up the OCTD public bus route that went into Santa Ana. No more than ten minutes up the road she spotted his ass on the bus. She started honking the horn and screaming at him to get off the bus. When the bus stopped, he got out and my mom beat him down! It was like seeing my dad in action all over again, but this time, it was my mom doing the ass kicking! I mean she fucked him up!! In all my life I have never seen a girl fight like a man until I saw my mom get down! He was screaming and pleading for her to stop, but she just kept going! My heart was beating so fast, and this shit was getting more and more intense! When she finally stopped punching, she looked him in the eye and then there was a brief pause. Then she cold-cocked him one last time right in the jaw!

Growing up I fuckin hated this man! He did a lot of shitty things to my mom and me. He always punked me around when my mom wasn't there. He was just an outright piece of shit. I don't care who reads this book and doesn't like it either. Would you go find yourself a thief, a liar, and a cheat, and expose him to your closest loved ones, the ones that you care the most about and would do anything for them? I would hope that your response to this is NO.

I have to tell you, though, fast forward ten years later that it was a sad day when the sheriff called to tell me that they found him dead in the laundry mat in Santa Ana where all of the hypes hung out. In my mind I imagined a man sitting on the toilette seat in a ghetto laundry mat restroom. He served himself a cocktail and then went to sleep and never woke up. That's what happens when you play the game. The game of life is fierce and that's why I play it like a playoff game. One wrong move and you will be eliminated. This is life when you decide to play games with it.

When the police asked us to come and identify the body, it was even sadder to see my mom cry, holding his cold, dead body and whispering the words, "I tried to help you."

The truth is we always try our best to help others, and about 98% of the time, we fail.

Change starts and ends with the individual. Only the individual can make the decision to get out of the old ways and into the new.

When he passed away, my twin brothers were only four years old and my sister was about ten. My sister did not cry at all. Looking back, I don't know if she was just hard-core from day one or if she just didn't care because he was in and out of jail and was never around.

The thing that stung the most on the day of that funeral was when we were leaving the church. I was holding my younger brother, Daniel's, hand. He looked up to me and said, "James...how come my dad isn't waking up, James? James?" Tears filled my eyes and my vision blurred, but I just kept walking. I didn't know what to say. There was no way to explain what had happened to a four year old boy.

Yeah, another scar on the heart. That was just what I needed.

<u>As a parent your job is to sacrifice your life for your family</u>. Anything less than 100% is not good enough. When 100% is not good enough, you put it in sixth gear and get that extra ten percent in to make things right!

Do whatever it takes!! Excuses are just excuses and are not acceptable!! My step-dad had three wonderful biological children and missed out on a great life because his drugs and his lifestyle were more important to him than his family was. The end for him was exactly what he asked for. You reap what you sow and others will, in fact, know you by the fruit that you bear. Everyone has a choice. **<u>We are where we are in life because we chose to be there.</u>**

Chapter 9: I'm Different

Even though we now resided in Costa Mesa in 1987, we still made trips to East Los Angeles and Pico Rivera every weekend. The majority of our family still lived in the LA County area.

Every trip back to Pico Rivera, I could tell that things just got worse. As I was adapting to the biggest culture shock in my life, those that I knew in LA were spiraling downhill fast.

When I visited my old friend Sergio in Pico Rivera, I was shocked when I asked about old friends that I used to hang out with on the playground. Little Frankie had been expelled from junior high school for selling weed and was now shooting up heroin in the seventh grade. My childhood crush, Rene, had paid the price for something that her uncles had done to a rival gang member. Rene had been spotted at a Jack in the Box somewhere in Montebello. The rival gang members followed her into the restroom and stabbed her several times, leaving her face sliced up beyond recognition. She had been so beautiful to me. Such a tragedy.

Now it doesn't take a rocket scientist to figure out that there would be massive bloodshed over this incident. This would ignite a war of families that would never die until the last family member on one side or the other was dead. This is a way of life for those who reside in that neck of the woods.

I always laughed at the OC boys when they talked about gang banging. My own personal experiences in Los Angeles far exceeded the level of violence in Orange County. I mean OC has occasional stabbings and a few deaths by gun shot, but in LA County people were dying every night. Homicide was life in that neck of the woods.

When I was about twenty-one years old, an elderly gentleman asked me, sarcastically, why I thought people lived that way and why would they think that that kind of lifestyle was okay. He was extremely wealthy and had grown up with a silver spoon in his mouth. My response to him was to never waste his time again on such subjects; he couldn't begin to understand. It is my belief that anyone who has never set foot in that type of environment would be incapable of comprehending the mindset of those who live out their daily lives in the inner cities of America. It's a different world out there, and the game of life is played by a whole different set of rules.

Chapter 10: Life Was Changing

My sister was born in 1987, and my life changed again. My step-dad was in and out of jail and mom was forced to raise us all on her own. I had to learn to be responsible real quick. At the age of ten, I was the man of the house. I was already cleaning our entire house, making dinner for us, doing my own laundry, ironing my own clothes, bathing and taking care of my little sister.

My grades in school were really poor, as I was not a very good student. I wasn't a bad kid. I just had too much shit going on at home, so I just couldn't really absorb what was being taught in school. As a matter of fact, when I got to O.C. those kids were very smart! I mean in L.A., we were still doing addition, subtraction, division and multiplication. The OC kids were already reading and doing math at the college level. So, long story short, I was put in what was called the RSP program. Real Stupid People is what the other students called the program. It was a program designed for kids who were behind in whatever curriculum everyone else was learning and I think I stayed in RSP until I was in the tenth grade.

Like I said, I had to grow up quick. My step-pops was no help to us at all. In fact, he was a prick to me when my mom wasn't around. He played the part well around other people, wondering out loud why I didn't like him, but he and I really knew what was going on. He was everything that I believed in life to be just shit. He was a terrible role model, a horrible husband and provider, and, in my own honest opinion, an absolute waste of space on this earth.

Men of my stature are extremely passionate about our families and will stop at nothing to provide all needs for them, regardless of the cost. With a "whatever it takes" mentality, that is exactly what I have dedicated my life to doing. When one of us is not happy it affects the whole tribe and as a leader of the tribe, it is my job to ensure all of their emotional and physical needs are met. This is the life of the selfless individual. We put others needs of whom we love before our own as this is the right thing to do. Leaders take everyone to the mountain top with them. If you stand at the mountain top alone, you are not a leader. You are simply just a mountain climber.

Chapter 11: The Power of The Mind

Today, at the age of forty, I WORK MY ASS OFF to provide for my family. My engine never stops. I never stop thinking of how I am going to get us to the next level in this life. I have dedicated my life to serving my family, my community, and my employees. I'm the kind of man that would have to be having a really fucked-up day to not take a dollar out of my pocket to feed a homeless man or woman begging for change on a street corner. My life traumatized me. I grew up around people who showed me by poor example that, if you stop improving and if you stop caring about life, not only will you be left behind, but you will be letting everyone else around you down. You will be a major disappointment to those who once looked up to you. And I refused to be that person.

I give thanks every day for my wife and children. I give thanks for my health. I even give thanks for the roof over my head and the warm, comfy bed that I wake up in every morning. Every year during the holidays we stand in a large circle and say a nice little prayer. After the prayer we go around the room and ask everyone to give thanks for something in their lives that they are grateful for. This year at Thanksgiving I was most grateful for a mind and soul that just will not quit! I don't know how to quit or give up. I don't stop until I get the results that I want.

The power of the mind is incredible. Anything that you set your mind to do can and will be accomplished. I am a true example of this. Not only did I achieve every goal that I have ever set in life, but I smashed the fuck out of every one of them. By doing that I even shocked the hell out of myself! This is how I know that the principle of hard work and dedication will never go unrewarded.

I developed a complex growing up. I always felt like a loser when I was young and it created a fire inside of me that one day turned in to a full blown inferno. I decided that my era of Merrifield would be far more greater than anyone could have ever imagined that it could ever be. I felt that the men with my last name did not do shit with it, and I was determined to be the one to elevate it. And I did.

The power of the mind is extremely mighty. So, guard your mind carefully and make sure that you only fill it with thoughts of greatness. You have to practice greatness daily. It will not just show up at your front door step. You have to go looking for it daily.

Chapter: 12 My Dad Let Go

It was about this time in my life when my dad had met another woman and decided that she and all her children would be his top priority. I went from seeing my dad on the weekend, to once a month, to once every six months, to once a year, to eventually not seeing him for years at a time. We were totally done as father and son.

When I was I kid I loved that man with all my heart. He was everything to me. It killed me that he just put me on the shelf like that and abandoned me. This was my first heartbreak in life, but it would not be the last.

The best memories I have with my dad were when I was a kid and I lived with both of my parents in Riverside. He used to take me hiking on the hills located on Arlington just off the 91 freeway. These were great bonding experiences as we would take our dogs with us and let them run wild up and down the mountain. On the way home, we would stop by a small ma and pa sandwich shop called "The Grinder." He would buy us both an Orange Crush soda, and then we would finish the short walk back home.

One of my best memories was the day my parents and I went to buy my dad some new work jeans. As we passed by a pet shop, this golden labrador puppy and I locked eyes, and I had to have that dog. My dad didn't get those jeans that day. Instead, I got a puppy. We named her Goldie Gold. That dog was most loyal to me and was always by my side. She even slept at the foot of my bed as my protector.

My dad leaving me is the biggest reason why I have dedicated my life to my family. It is because I know what it feels like to be left alone in a cold-blooded world, abandoned by the one you loved the most. My children have been the focal point of my life since day one. Being a father and watching them grow is one of the best experiences that I could have ever been given the opportunity to experience. It's like starting a garden when you know very little about taking care of crops. What you do know for sure is that you must protect them, you must look after them constantly, you must love what you are doing, and you must dedicate your life to the farming. The same is also true when you are raising kids. They must be your life's entire focal point.

Chapter 13: Making Friends

Let's just say that I wasn't a fan of school. Like I already said, I did not fit in and I didn't have any friends. The kids of OC treated me like shit and did everything that they could to make me feel unwelcomed.

My job was to get out of school each day, so that I could go home and take care of my little sister, make dinner, and keep the house in order. That was my job.

At the age of twelve, I took pride in doing my job well. I was a damn good supporting cast member. This is where I first learned that TEAM was essential and that team starts in the home! Team is everything!!

Since I didn't have very many friends, my cousins Mark and Chris were the closest friends that I had. Mark was the comedian and was extremely sharp with the ladies. Me and Mark were very close in our younger years. Chris was more on the sensitive side. Because Mark and I loved to clown and talk a lot of shit, cousin Chris was always mad at us. We still loved him. All I know is the three of us cousins loved to be together.

I spent many summers with Mark and eventually spent most of my teen age years with Chris too as they both came to live with us in Costa Mesa. I had loved them since we were kids. We did everything together. We would go to the beach every day. We smoked weed every day and drank forty once bottles of old English 800 Malt Liquor in the alleys. They were my cousins and were the closest things that I had to brothers when I was growing up.

In seventh grade, I started making friends in my neighborhood. I met this girl named Dorothy. She was a white girl chola who would end up being one of my closest lifelong friends. Dorothy was raised by a single dad, who I would later become very close to. They were extremely well off, and when you grew up with very minimal funds, you kind of gravitate towards people like that. They had a sick house in Costa Mesa with a custom kitchen, custom restrooms, a billiard room, and a really nice sun deck with a custom jacuzzi. All my favorite things were in that house. Her father, Mr. Stoll, loved me and treated me very well. He would buy me breakfast daily and take me to school. He was the first person who ever told me that, if you love what you do, then you will never have to work another day of your life. He always kept it positive for me, and he was always good to me.

Dorothy caught a lot of shit because she was a white girl chola. She was a gangster chick who wore black corduroy pants with a clean, crisp well-ironed white sweater. Her black eyeliner was very thick and her make-up was packed on like bondo. She was already affiliated with some of the gang bangers from both OC and LA. Back then in Costa Mesa, that white girl chola shit was frowned upon, but I didn't give a fuck. Dorothy was my friend. She was one of my very first real friends, and when it came to trust and loyalty, I was the dude that you wanted on your side when the shit went down. We had each other's back big time. We became family. On Fridays her dad would drop us off at a place called Skate Ranch in Santa Ana California. Dorothy was a state wide roller skating champion. The girl could jam out really hard on roller skates. I wasn't much of a skater. But Dorothy would not allow me to stand on the wall and not do shit. When the couples skating song would come on and the lights would go low, she would grab me by the hand and say "lets go." She taught me how to roller skate.

About a year later, I met the group of neighborhood guys who would eventually become my lifelong friends. Maui, David, and Joey were now in my life and they were the first guy friends I had ever had outside of family. Maui was like the Eazy E of our group. He was always dressed in the finest gangster gear. He wore a black Los Angeles Kings Starter Jacket and a Black LA Raiders baseball cap to match. His father owned his own business, so naturally Maui just gravitated towards entrepreneurship at a very young age. David ended up being my best friend. He and I had a relationship that was very special. David and I were inseparable and I called him "brother." David had my back and I had his. Joey was tall and handsome. All the chicks loved Joey. He was indeed a ladies' man. To this day I am still close to Maui and Joey. David is now living overseas and can never return to the United States, but that is a whole different story. I miss David with all of my heart. He and I had a very special brotherhood. It is my belief that God puts people in your life for a reason. Why He takes them away, I will never understand.

Chapter 14: A Lot Less Tolerant of Bullshit

At this point of my life, after seeing my mom go through all the drama with my step-dad, my real dad just quit on me, I can honestly say that I just wanted out. I wanted a better life. The bottom line is that I just wanted to be happy and I wasn't getting that happiness at home. So, I found happiness in the streets.

Parents your children will go to various extremes to find the things that you are not providing for them in the home. I've heard every excuse in the book as to why parents cannot be there for their kids; such as I work too much, I don't have time, I'm tired. Well let me tell you that it's much easier to raise a child right the first time versus spending a life time trying to repair one.

You have a choice.

It is my belief that building a solid foundation begins in your home. Building a team atmosphere begins in your home. Love at its very best begins in your home. If you cannot fulfill this part of YOUR RESPONSIBILITY, you are operating a failing family program.

Before you know it, I was getting high daily with Maui, David, Joey, and my cousins Mark and Chris. When we hit the ninth grade everything really changed. I was no longer some quiet, insecure, reserved individual. Those days were long gone. Maui bought his first car and the boys were rolling. Maui was notorious for having the monster bumps (sound system) in his car. You could hear us driving down the block and you knew exactly who it was.

I was given the nick name Big Chunk, and it stuck to me like glue. Everywhere I went people at one point only knew me as Chunk and not by my real name. It was one of the most glorious times of my life, and it only got better. Now I had a lot of friends and we were partying it up on the regular. I just had this overflowing amount of confidence that I had never had before. I had never been so happy in my life. Life outside my home was fuckin great! I felt like a totally different person.

From that point on, all I wanted to do is be out in the streets. The street is where people like me turned for love. This is why it is so critical for families to be rooted in love because the fact is that WE ALL NEED LOVE and we will go to major extremes to get it. My circle just kept getting bigger and bigger. For the first time in my life, I had finally found a happy place. I finally had friends. Friends who accepted me for who I was. I didn't have to pretend to be someone I wasn't just to fit in. My speech was vulgar, and my presence was strong. To me life could not be any better. I was in a better place in my life as my life revolved around my friends, music, and getting stoned.

Chapter 15: The Party Continues

Sophomore year rolled around, and the partying just kept getting stronger and stronger. By now everyone knew who I was. My core group of friends and I had established ourselves in our city.

As the party scene continued, we figured out the art of hustling and selling dope. We were no longer just looking to score twenty-dollar bags of weed. We were now in the game of selling it. As a youngster, I always looked up to my older cousins in LA and in the "Inland Empire," or IE, as they were heavily involved in the dope trade. Now it was our turn to get our feet wet. Little did we realize that we would be opening a can of worms that would leave some of us scarred for life.

An OG named Jimbo from 76st East Coast Crips in South Central Los Angeles moved in next door to us and showed us how to weigh up and sell dope. Jimbo grew up in the day of Monster Cody and Tookie Williams. He knew them both on a first name basis. Research these men. They were stone-cold killers from the 70s and 80s. Jimbo taught us all about dope quality and pricing. The guy was a bonafide hustler, and we all looked up to him. He was about twenty-five years older than us at the time. Some dudes just can't leave the game alone and will stay dedicated to it their whole lives. They wind up being the corrupters of our youth and perpetuating the cycle.

By this time, a few more guys had joined our click, but one in particular was our home boy, Ewa. Ewa and I had an instant connection. It was like a brotherhood that was meant to be. We met in between classes at school, and, within minutes, we were getting high together. He became part of our immediate circle, and I would call him brother along with the rest of the gang. We lived on a street called Coolidge in Costa Mesa. It was one of three run down areas of Costa Mesa at the time. In all these areas, you were sure to find us and the drugs. Still I was enjoying my life. I was enjoying my company. I was enjoying being young and fearless. Life was great and a whole new ball game was being played on our block.

Batter up.

Keep in mind that, even though I was enjoying life, I was still an angry teenager. Anger had really taken hold of my heart and my mind and now it was time to release it on the regular. If you had been through all the bullshit that I had gone through when I was a kid, then would you understand my life and the way I felt. My dad leaving me out to dry was really fucking up my head. My step-dad and his heroin addiction also took a toll on me. He and my mom would stay up all night long and fight like cats and dogs. Screaming, cussing, and breaking shit. The thought of these men not giving my mom or us kids a good life sucked and I became a hungry lion out on the streets, constantly looking for a meal.

Anyone who stepped out of line was getting fucked up, and there would be no mercy granted. I do recall beating MEN—not kids my age—but MEN, down to the point of leaving them in the streets unconscious. That was my outlet for releasing anger. It just felt so good. It felt so right. All the years of being a victim were now over, and I felt that it was time to avenge myself. No one would ever hurt me again. No one would ever get the best of me, and no one would get away with trying to fuck with me or any of my people because, by now, we had started carrying guns and were not afraid to use them. We were young and now very dangerous.

Chapter 16: Heather

By the time junior year came, a lot had changed. Our crew was now divided in half. As meth amphetamine rocked the nation, so it also wrecked our crew. By this time, I was rolling mostly with Ewa and David. David came to live with us when his dad went back to Argentina and left him behind. He was my comrade. We would experience many things growing up together. If it was anyone I am glad that it was him.

The block was infested with drugs and it seemed that our crew had turned its back on one another. I'm a power player, so naturally I clicked up with a few power players from the West Side of town. These guys were about four years older and were heavily involved in crime on a different level. (To protect the past of these men, I will not be mentioning any of their names.) I also clicked up with a few of my boys from the CMHS football team. The party must go on right? Why stop now? Little did I know it was all about to change. That year, I met the woman who would end up being the mother of my two oldest children and a life-long pain in my ass.

I still remember the day that she walked in to my driver's ed class. She was beautiful, about 5 feet 8 inches tall, with long blond hair, green eyes, pale white skin, and a pretty smile. That day she walked in the class about ten minutes late and just stood in the door way. It was magic as we just stared at each other. She and I had a bond that was really strong. We just could not stay away from each other. She would take her mom's car at night, so that she could go to ROP and would ditch her night classes to come down to Coolidge Street to be with me. We would hang out in the front of my apartment until it was time for her to go, and after that, we would talk on the phone for hours. She was my partner in crime. Looking back at those high school days, we had some good times together. I was really in to Heather and she was in to me. She wasn't a power player. In fact she was kind of a loner. But I liked that. It meant that she wasn't all damaged property and wasn't tied in to anyone that I knew.

Though I experienced division amongst my friends that year, I had started a new relationship elsewhere with Heather. I guess that's the story of life. You make room for new beginnings when old relationships come to an end. In my case, this year of change would end on a bad note.

Watch your step.

One night I was hanging out with a mix of twenty of my old friends from the block and a few other new partners from the West Side at the HIGH HOUSE, which was just a few apartments next door from where I lived. We had few cases of Old English 800 Malt and a few ounces of the Chronic. Once again, it was on. That night it was decided that everyone was going to drop an acid tab. Acid is a hallucinogen that will make you see things that are not real, kind of like that Jimmy Hendricks experience type shit. I wasn't about to fuck with it. I had tried it in the tenth grade, and it scared shit out of me. That night the rule was that if you were not going to drop, then you would have to leave. When they made the call saying it was time to get high, I said "Fuck You" with authority! Nobody could tell me what the fuck to do! I looked to my best friend David and said, "Let's go!" But Dave looked and me and replied, "I'm staying Chunk." I looked at David with disgust and walked out the door. Out of the entire party, I was the only one who left. I was the only one who decided to not do acid that night. Standing alone in the alley way I lit a joint and started walking home. That night I just stayed in my room and passed out with the television on.

The next day, I realized that David never made it home, so I set out to look for him. I started making phone calls to see if I could find David and the news that I got was devastating. One of the older homies from the West told me that my homeboy had been acting like a little bitch that night. He said that, when the acid kicked in, David had stayed in the corner, scared to death, and would not come out. That night I knew that something bad was going to happen. In that era a few of our acquaintances had some bad experiences where some of these people got permanent brain damage from doing acid. After experiencing acid once I knew that that shit was not for me.

I immediately hung up the phone and drove around the block in search of my brother. I drove to the parks and to every one of our friends' houses. I finally found him at his girlfriend's house. When we locked eyes, the look of connection we had always had was gone, replaced by fear and confusion. David knew that something was wrong with him; he could not snap out of his current mental state of mind. He had fried his brain on acid and would never be the same again. Re-living this event is very painful for me.

Kids, please do not ever fuck around with synthetic drugs. These drugs will destroy your life forever. Once the damage has been done, you cannot wish your way out of it. You do not get a re-do. No!! You are fucked for life!! The entire course of your life will change for the worse and you will now be an example for all to see. You will be an example of what not to be. What not to do. What not to follow. For the next few years after that David was in and out of jail, and around four years later, David would end up getting deported back to Argentina for his crimes.

Chapter 17: Senior year! Time To Ball Out!

I was playing football, selling dope, and kicking ass in the streets. Every Friday night we had a party to go to. I just couldn't lose!! Life was great, and I was enjoying every minute of it! The energy in my city was so magical. I can honestly say that my freshman and senior year in high school were the absolute best days of my teen age life. So full of adventure and new things. So full of real life just happening at the speed of light. All I wanted to do was hang out with my friends, ditch class, party, go to the beach, and just live!

I was spending more time with my girlfriend, Heather, as the two of us grew very close. I started to drift away from the homies on my block. Now I spent a lot more of my time with a few of my team mates Junior and Jason. Junior grew up on El Camino Street, which was one of the three fucked up neighborhoods in our city. Jason came to our high school my junior year. He was just a sophomore when we met him. I spent a lot of time with Jason and Junior. We called ourselves The Wolfpack. Wolves are vicious animals and are always hungry for destruction. The pack was into kicking ass too. We used to show up to parties and beat other dudes up all the time just because we could. We were strong and very confident in our abilities to walk away as winners. On top of that, my new clique from the West Side had my back strong too. Yup you guessed it...we were UNTOUCHABLE! Very untouchable.

As the year came to an end, I graduated from high school and the Army came knocking at my door. They wanted me to join, and I got really serious about it, but after they said that I needed to lose 150 pounds, I said, "Fuck that. I'm just going to sell dope and stay here in Costa Mesa."

Chapter 18: Summer 1995

The year before 1994 my mom gave birth to my twin brothers Daniel and Raymond. The twins were a blast and we really enjoyed them as it is very rare for a woman to give birth to multiples at one time. We now had twins in our immediate family. We nick named them Snoop and Dre. Dan was little and skinny so he was Snoop and Ray was chunky so we called him Dre. Me, Chris, Mark, and David chipped in on the regular to help raise them. Of course their good for nothing father wasn't around very much. He was still roaming the streets on heroin, still going in and out of jail. But together me and my cousins along with best friend David just made it work. We were excited to have a new set of boys in the family. We would get stoned and then go to back yard with the twins and teach them how to shoot free throws and how to hit and catch a baseball. This is what you do with kids when they are little to develop there little minds. You spend as much quality time with them as you can. These were good times. There is beauty in the struggle. It's up to you to find it. No matter what the circumstances were we just always seemed to make it work. I guess that's what you have to do when life throws you a lemon. You make that lemonade as best as you can and enjoy it.

That summer the block got hot with the drugs and the violence. We weren't just beating each other up any more. We were now shooting at each other. My old crew quickly banded back together as we needed each other to stay alive. Costa Mesa was getting ugly.

I remember the day my mother reamed me a new one because my twin brothers were in my room and found my 30/30 lever action rifle next to my bed. I was pissed that they were in my room, but I still owned up to it. I fucked up; the gun should not have been there. Mom stuck my ass on a plane to Hawaii to stay with my aunt and uncle for about thirty days. When I came back, she had already bounced off Coolidge Street and had moved us up out of the block and to nicer residence.

After that life got real weird. This new neighborhood was nice and clean and was pretty much very boring. Then my mom brought my grandma to live with us and that was no fun. Grandma tripped out and made a scene every time Cousin Chris and I got stoned. I just fucked around and did nothing until about October of that year. That was the year that my girlfriend became pregnant with our first child—Ashley Marie Merrifield.

Honestly the thought of being a dad really didn't phase me. I wasn't scared. I figured since I helped raise my baby sister and twin baby brothers I would do just fine at raising my own child. My journey as a parent was about

64

to begin. I was still a wild immature animal, but there is no way that I would back down from owning up to my responsibilities. No way.

Chapter 19:

You Gotta Start to Grow Up Sometime...

I know. This is where you think the story gets boring. Well, think again because shit just kept getting more real for James Merrifield.

Stay tuned and pay close attention.

In 1996, I watched my girlfriend walk through her graduation ceremony with a big belly that was ready to burst. My baby girl, Ashley Marie Merrifield, was born a week later. Instantly, I fell in love. Now, keep in mind that my lifestyle hadn't changed much. I was still getting high every day. Staying up all night. Sleeping all day. Still hustling out in the streets trying to get mine.

At the same time, reality hit quick because I was now a father. My Uncle Greg was constantly beating on me, saying, "What the heck are you going to do, James?!!! You know you have to get a freaking job now, right?!! You can't just keep living the way you are living!!! So, what are you going to do!!!!??"

The truth is, at eighteen years old I didn't know what I was going to do. The very next day I looked in the mail and found the Penny Saver. If you are way too young to know what the Penny Saver was, it was like this free classified ad newspaper that was delivered by snail mail once a week to your front door step.

I turned to the front page and it said, "Now looking for baggers at Albertson's in Irvine." There it was!! That is where the new journey began.

I started at the very bottom as a bagger making $5.45 an hour at Albertson's in Irvine, California. Now, keep in mind that $5.45 an hour doesn't pay for shit. As a matter of fact, after I saw my first full 40+ hour week paycheck after taxes was about $180.00. I went straight to the dope man, bought a half ounce and flipped it about ten times. I wasn't going to be able to walk away from the hustle just yet. In fact, once I built a network in that Albertson's building, I had all the managers buying dope from me. I even got to drink at the local dive bar with the veterans and would come back to work from lunch all buzzed. No one could tell me shit because they were all buying dope from me and I owned their asses. Now every Friday was a big pay day for me.

Chapter 20: My First Mentor

After about almost a year of bagging groceries, I became very interested in learning how to manage the business and was promoted to work the deli department, and within a few months, became an assistant deli manager. I showed up to work every day and kept a solid work ethic. No matter what you think of me after reading my book up to this point and TO THIS VERY DAY, my work ethic is extremely strong. No matter what, I showed up on time for every shift. I was learning to become a dedicated soldier who would some day lead the entire operation at store level, and that deli experience really taught me a lot. I learned how to write an order and take inventory. I learned about gross profit margin. I was already good at math because I was acclimated to maximizing profit margins from selling dope. This was a good learning ground and, on top of that, I met a good solid group of core people that would end up being lifelong friends. Even better, I met my first mentor.

This man stood about six feet tall and weighed a good 260 pounds. He had a cold stare and, for the most part, kept everyone in check. He was the bottom line authority in that building, and if you fucked around, he would surely hold you accountable for it. No one would dare test his authority. For whatever reason, he and I seemed to gravitate towards each other. One thing that I did know for sure was that, for the first time in my life, I had met a man who I would someday want to emulate. I had never had a male role model in my life like him, and when I found out that he made about 150 thousand a year to run the grocery store, I knew that this would be me someday. I now had my first real goal and most important I know had my first mentor. Thank God for the mentors of the world. Without mentors we are all a bunch of boats stranded at sea with no paddles. With no mentor in your life it is merely impossible to go to the places of the unknown. If you want to elevate your life and the lives of those closest to you it is my belief that you must first find a mentor. It must be someone who has proven results in the field of your interest and will be able to lead you to the place that you have always dreamed of going.

Since then he and I have worked for four different companies together. In fact, he is the former Western Vice President of the company that we both work for today. No doubt we have all come a very long way in life. I am very grateful that God placed this man in my life. He was a major blessing in disguise as I truly believe that I would not have made it this far in life without his leadership.

Chapter 21:

Along the Way, Things Still Get Rocky

By the time of Ashley's first birthday, my girlfriend and I were drifting apart. She had started cheating on me with another dude at her work. I was really saddened by this because I really loved her, but when that kind of bs starts going down, it will fuck with your head a little…or a lot. For the second time in my life, I was heartbroken. Not too long after that, in 1997, my step- dad died from a heroin overdose, and a few months later we lost our house and became homeless. My mother went back to Pico Rivera where she stayed with my twin baby brothers and my little sister. I was taking twelve units at Orange Coast College in Business Administration and working forty + hours a week at Albertson's in Irvine.

All of this happened so fast and I just could not get my arms around the situation fast enough.

But I got very lucky because my old friend, Matt Metoyer's, mom Char let my cousin Black C and me stay at their side house for a while. Char was a life saver. Trust me. After my bad break up, my step-dad dying, everyone now having to scatter and find a place to live, I was most grateful for Char's kind heart. Today, Char sits on a School Board of Directors in Costa Mesa. She spoke this year at my son Cody's graduation. During her speech I could not help but be proud and reminisce, thinking that that woman standing behind the microphone allowed me to sleep, shower, do laundry, and eat in her home. These are the true heroes in this world. These are the true difference makers. Of course, I could not stay there forever, but I am very grateful for Char's beautiful heart.

Things were tough for us all, but it really hurt me the most to see my mother regress. She didn't know what to do. It's like she was being delivered right back to the old life where we came from. But what could I do? Sometimes I would pull over and park my car next to the old park on Coolidge Street and fall asleep there because I was so tired from school and a 48 hour work week. Life was really fucked up then. I lived in survival mode, and that is when your mind is at its peak performance in terms of "living for the day." In my mind I was just telling myself to "keep on pushing through." "It's going to be ok." "And Just keep on doing your best."

Just do your best…

I had always been in the gym since my freshman year in high school, but now I went hard core to the extreme. I started pumping iron more seriously than ever. I needed an outlet for my stress and my anger.

Within about ten months of pumping iron and doing cardio a good six days a week, I slimmed down from 310 pounds to 210 pounds and was rock-motherf'n-solid!! I felt great!! Health wise, I felt wonderful, and in my mind I felt really good, but deep down inside I still missed my girlfriend. We started to talk again and, little by little, she started to make her way back into my life. Before you know it, we were back together. I wanted us to be a family for Ashley. I really cared about her and wanted a good life for all of us.

The guy who she left me for wasn't too happy about that and told me that he was going to come to the house after work and kick my ass. He had no idea who he was fucking with. In my mind I had killed him over and over again. He was about to take a trip in to the dark side.

I could have sent someone to take care of him when she first started messing around with him, but I didn't. When your woman cheats on you, she is the one to blame. Not the other man. If a woman is truly faithful, she will never allow another man to be comfortable enough to get that close to her.

Well, anyway, that night I staged an ambush. As he pulled up in his cheap little car, I had some of my player partners posted up on the street corner waiting for him. He never saw it coming. Not only did he get the shit knocked out of him, but his car was missing all the windows and the exterior would never look the same. I stood in the shadows with my life long crime partner and watched the entire thing unfold. I wasn't looking on as a cheering squad. See I'm more like a boss and a boss watches his people do the work for him. Never under estimate the power of one. I am sure that this man thought that, because I was five years younger than he was, he wouldn't have any problems dealing with me. He thought that I was just some punk ass kid. He was wrong. I must admit that I enjoyed my authority and was not afraid to use it.

After my girlfriend and I reconciled, I had a difficult time forgiving her for cheating on me. I just could not forget the past. In my mind I felt very insecure and the thought was that since it had already happened once, it would probably happen again. Right? Still, I continued to work hard for us both on and off the field. There was nothing that I would not do for my family. We moved in to a two bed room apartment together and I was trying to start my family life.

After a few short years at Albertson's, I became very unhappy with my immediate supervisor and ended up walking off the job. I then went to work for Trader Joe's. I got screwed out of a few quarters an hour at Trader Joe's and wasn't too thrilled about that. I was now working nights and wasn't a happy about that either, but I stayed true to the game and kept selling dope. By now, I was very good at it. My cousins in LA and in IE helped me a lot as they were hard-core affiliated with the dudes that were bringing in bricks from across the border. I was buying kilos of marijuana for $300.00 a pop. The only catch was that, for that low price, I had to buy ten kilos at a time. No problem, right? When you have a vision, there are no limits to what your mind can do. I had solid STAR in my area of Southern California. Every corner of the star represents a certain individual who controls the drug trade in a certain city or county. These individuals moved all of the weight for me. I was just the dude who had the connections for mass quantities and the best prices on purchasing in bulk.

Fast forward to today Marijuana is legal in several states. And guess who saw the opportunity in the taxation of these goods? That's right, you guessed it; The Government of the United States of America. After all this is the land of the free and the home of the brave…right?

I had gone from nickels to dimes to quarters to ounces to pounds to now selling kilos.

Chapter 22: June 23rd 1998

It was about midnight and I had just gotten off work. The day before, an old friend had sold me a 12 gauge pistol grip pump shotgun for fifty bucks, and that night I was in a gun cleaning mood. I always kept my guns well-oiled and cleaned up.

I was still angry about working nights at my new job and taking a fifty cent per hour pay cut. In the comfort of my new apartment, I decided to light up a joint, get stoned, and oil up that 12 gauge pistol grip pump when out of nowhere I heard a knock at the door. Keep in mind that I just had my young bloods knock the shit out of my girlfriend's ex or whatever you want to call him. I never underestimated anyone, so I turned off all the lights and went backwards out onto the patio with a few nitro mags in my shotgun ready to kill at will. As I moved out of the sliding glass window to the patio area, I saw who was at the front door. It was my best friend Ewa. He was beaten very badly and could not even speak. He had blood coming out of his nose, his ears, and even out of his eyes. My first instinct was payback and right then and there, I knew that someone was going to get fucked up tonight. Ewa had been with some of the younger homies that night. They had been cruising down a side street when someone in a large group threw a bottle at the car that they were riding in and, like a bunch of fucking idiots, they turned around and went back only to find that they were outnumbered five to one.

I went outside and told the other youngsters all to leave at once. They were not very happy with me because they had come to "Big Chunk" for back up. These little boys were not ready for the major leagues just yet, and I was up to bat with the bases loaded.

I immediately packed my new shot gun and my 40 mm. I grabbed the black ski mask and Ewa and I headed out the door. Somebody was going to pay for what they had done to Ewa. To this day, the visual of his face that night still hurts my heart. Vengeance was now on the horizon. You don't go making a mad man even madder. And you for damn sure better be extra cautious in this day and age because what you think is funny could very easily trigger the wrong person off and the consequences can be very severe.

I will leave out the details as you can only imagine what happened, but what happened next will blow your mind.

After the deed was done, we raced to the freeway. I was about 500 feet from the freeway entrance when I realized that I had forgot to turn the lights on. The next thing I know, I saw red and blue lights behind me. I immediately screamed to Ewa to put the guns under the seat! I'm cussing up a storm yelling, "We're going down bro! We are going down!" I told Ewa to lie down in the back seat and pretend to be asleep.

Next, I pulled the car over.

As the cop walked up to the side of the car, I told myself, *It's game time* and *I am going home to sleep in my own bed tonight*. The officer asked me if I knew why he pulled my over. I replied that I did not believe that I was going too fast. He said that it was because my head lights were not on as I was rolling up to the freeway. I began to give a fake laugh and told him that I did, in fact, realize that my lights were not on when I was almost at the freeway. He asked what I was doing out so late and I told him that my brother in the back seat had had too much to drink and I wanted to get him home safely, so I went to pick him up from a local dive bar.

The cop flashed his lights in Ewa's face and, at that moment, Ewa turned actor and gave an Oscar-winning performance, as well. Ewa opened his eyes and said, "Oh, Oh, what's going on!?" and I very gently replied to him, "Relax brother. Everything is okay."

My devilish mind went to work and asked the clean-cut rookie cop if my friend from the gang unit was working tonight and that is when he broke. He was ultra fuckin excited that I knew his sergeant and mentor. Knowing that I had this rookie policeman wrapped around my finger, I fed him a few bullshit lines. He then proceeded to run a check on my license plates. I still remember as he walked away how Ewa was in the back seat whispering the Hail Mary Prayer. LMFAO!! I do recall telling him to STFU, as I was about to finish the game. The cop came back to state that my license was still suspended, which it was, and said that because I was so cool I could just leave my car on the side street and walk the rest of the way home. Without hesitation, I took the deal. Game over.

Chapter 23: TRUE STORY!!!

The very next day was the day of my daughter Ashley's second birthday party.

Our kids' birthday parties are always huge!! This party was at the park next to our house and we were about a good sixty friends and family deep. I grilled hamburgers and hot dogs for everyone, but that day, as I stood there at the grill, something really strange happened to me. Something went off inside my soul. My mind blanked out and tunnel vision set in. It was my conscience. It began to speak to me. It had never been there before, but at that moment it was in full effect and it was scolding the shit out of me! It was saying, "Alright, fucker!! You're almost twenty-one years old and that shit is not going to fly anymore!! You cannot go running around in the streets any more like a fuckin' hoodlum trying to save all of your lame ass fuckin homies!! What happened last night must never happen again!!" Do you understand!!??"

Real talk.....No bullshit...that really happened.

After that day I never took the guns out of the house ever again. I realized that I could have done some serious prison time for some shit that I didn't even have anything to do with. And the worst part of it all was, what would have happened to Heather and Ashley? At that point I knew that I needed to wise up. With penalties being very severe in that era for violence of any kind it was time to settle down.

Not too long after Ashley turned two years old, Heather was pregnant again. This time, I married her. The wedding was small and very nice. We couldn't really afford a big wedding or a honey moon, but I do remember going home with a beer buzz that night. We sat in the living room and opened our wedding gifts. It was a good night as I still recall putting together a bar-b-que that night. How ironic! LOL. I was determined to be a great provider for this family. I would do anything for them. I would ensure that all their needs were fulfilled. My wife had had a very bad childhood, as well. That was one thing that we both had in common. When she was eight years old, her father died from a heroin overdose. She always spoke of how she loved her father with all her heart and that she was his special little angel. She said that he was a "controlled" heroin addict, meaning that he wasn't some low life like my step-father, who would go around stealing from everyone to support his habit. Her father was very stealthy about what he did. Most people were not aware of his addiction. He worked a full-time job and was a provider for his kids until the day that he passed. My wife was a big piece of my heart, and I was determined to give her a good life. I wanted to see her have all the nice things that my mom never had. I wanted to be that backbone that would carry an entire family on the weight of its shoulders. I was just in love with being in love. When you came from a few broken homes like I did, love is essential. Love is everything and I had to have it in my home.

Four months after we married on September 16, 1999 my son, Cody James Merrifield, was born. A super star was born! I was so very proud of him. It was love at first sight. I had known all along that he was going to be a boy! This father and son relationship would be the absolute greatest bond that I ever had in all my life! I wanted to be the best dad that I could possibly be—the best mentor, the best coach, the best friend. That is what I strived for. Together me and this kid were destined for greatness! After being exposed to a few worthless men in my life, I knew that my life objective was to break the cycle and create a better Merrifield than ever before! Life was changing for me and I embraced every minute of it! I knew that my life was only going to get better because now I had created the family that I always wanted when I was growing up.

I took my kids everywhere. Every day we were off work, we went to the park, fed the ducks, played on the swings, and went down the slides forever! In the summer time, we went swimming at the pool or at the beach every single day. Ashley and Cody were and still are two of the absolute biggest blessings that I have had in my life. Without these kids, I would be no one!! They made me who I am today! They were my biggest motivation to never give up on ANYTHING that held great value in my life.

Six months after Cody was born, shit started going downhill with my family. My cousin Joey got locked up for thirteen years on some really bad shit. Shortly after that, my cousin Memo died from a heart complication. He was just twenty-six years old. To make matters even worse, my cousin Davie, who was our leader and my biggest connect in East Los Angeles, got popped with some real dope and was going to do some very hard prison time.

I told myself to chill the fuck out and stop selling dope. Too many bad things were happening around me and I felt like the walls were closing in on me. But the truth is that I just couldn't stop…really even if I wanted to, I was not financially set to just give up the game. I had already established my side business in the dope trade and there was just way too much money being left on the table. I couldn't stay away. My normal job only paid me thirteen dollars an hour at the time. You can't raise and service a family of four on thirteen bucks an hour. I wish that I knew another way. But I didn't.

Still, as a few years passed, I continued to work my ass off in the grocery industry in hopes that someday all my hard work would pay off and I would never have to sell dope again. Little by little, I was starting to mature. My brain was working overtime trying to figure this thing out. I knew that I had to go legit. I was looking for that doorway of opportunity to do just that.

Chapter 24: Bad Card

Normally when you least expect it, that's when a major setback or something tragic takes place in your life. Like Curtis Blow said "These are the breaks". Now I was about to get mine.

When Heather was twenty-five, she got a job as an apartment manager in Anaheim, California. I wasn't too thrilled about moving to Anaheim, but she sold me on the idea that we would get free rent and could save some serious money so that we could save up and buy a home, so I took her up the deal and we relocated.

We moved to Anaheim and, within a short period of time, she began acting strangely. I started to feel awkward as I could tell that something was not right. She didn't want to have much to do with me anymore, and right away I became suspicious. Heather began to take a class in managing apartments and came home one day after getting her little bullshit apartment manager certification. She told me that she didn't need me anymore and wanted me to leave. I was shocked that this was happening. I mean just like that, she flipped her switch and made up her mind that we would go our separate ways? Really? No. Fuck that! She had been planning this move for a while! I ragged and asked her why in the fuck didn't she say that she felt this way before we left Costa Mesa? Why did she pull this stunt move and just leave me out to dry like that! Real talk ladies and gentlemen, she had a game plan and I was not a part of it. Keep in mind that this woman never had a job a day in her life. My earned income was our entire financial support. She now had a free rent pass and even got a little salary out of the deal. So foolishly she felt that she could conquer the world all by herself.

I knew that she was up to no good when, a few weeks later, she refused to let me go with her to her new boss's Christmas Party. That night, she got all dressed up to go out and left her wedding ring at home. She was having an affair with the maintenance man who was in charge of fixing everything at the apartments that her boss owned. It had happened again. This time she not only screwed me and the kids out of having a family, but now she began to drink heavily and started using synthetic drugs. She developed an addiction that she could not control. All those drugs and alcohol were a bad combination. I drove to the urgent care that she would get her pills from and begged the doctor to stop giving her the prescriptions. I begged and pleaded my case and told him that this was ruining my family! She was driving around town like a fuckin zombie under the influence of that shit with my kids in the car! I couldn't stop her. She was on a path to self-destruction and there was nothing that I could do to prevent her for doing that. I don't know what went off in her brain and possessed her to do this to us, but it happened. The roller coaster ride was about to get really, really rough as my biggest concerns were my kids.

Ironically, my ex-wife at one time was the leader of the JUST SAY NO CLUB. She NEVER did drugs or had a desire to party. She once told me when the kids were just little babies that she did not care what I did—since we met I had been a stoner. I had been hustling, and I wasn't much of a drinker. She said it didn't matter what I did, but that she felt that it was a mother's responsibility to stay sober and take care of the kids.

That made sense to me. After all, her dad had died of a heroin over dose when she was little and that scarred her for life. On top of that her mother was a swinger who loved to dabble in the cocaine. Yet, here she was, following the family tradition.

I had worked unselfishly for all of us. I gave my all to this woman and I only wanted to see her have the nice things that my mother didn't have. All my hard work just went to shit. I always believed that she and I would grow old together and would be as one for the rest of our lives. Now all I could do was watch her crash and burn at a rapid pace.

She was gone.

Chapter 25: Back to LA for a Minute

I moved to Montebello, California with mom and her old man Jesse. They were living in South Side Montebello which is a city that connects to East Los Angeles.

Less than a year after my step-dad overdosed, my mom met an OG from Nor Cal Flats through some mutual friends. This man would later step up and love my mother and my younger siblings as if they were his very own. Jesse provided for them until the day he died of cancer in 2011. Jesse was not just a good man. Jesse was a great man. Since his death life was never the same for my mom, my brothers, or my sister.

I was commuting for work back and forth from Irvine to Montebello. My first mentor and I hooked back up and we opened a grocery store together in Irvine for a group of wealthy Turkish millionaires. I worked six days a week for eighteen months on this project. At the time, the Turkish owners were the number one distributor of rice and tea in the nation. They handed over ten million dollars to us and told us to get this grocery store operation going. Today that store just celebrated its fifteenth year anniversary and does about one million dollars a week in sales. Talk about a great investment.

Though I was getting on my feet financially, this was a depressing time for me. Not only was I heartbroken about the situation with my wife, but I wasn't seeing my kids everyday like I was used to. I remember driving home from work and getting stoned the entire ride home with a forty ounce bottle of Old English 800 Malt Liquor in my lap and an attitude of "fuck the world!" My anger had returned and was burning a hole in my heart. Thoughts of hatred ruled my mind and soul. Once again I was in full blown survival mode.

I just didn't give a fuck. Life was terrible, and I had no way to escape reality other than to get loaded daily. My hair began to fall out rapidly from the stress. My nerves were shot. Out of good faith, I walked in to Grant's Guns, located in Costa Mesa, and sold my entire arsenal of legal weapons for cash. After that, I sold all my burners right back to the streets. I absolutely hated life, and I did not feel good about myself anymore. I sold those guns, not because I was afraid that I would hurt myself, but because I was afraid of getting revenge on the mother fucker who ruined my family. Had I killed his ass and gone to prison, my kids would be the ones who would suffer the most. At this point, without me in their life, they would be doomed. I know they needed me and I would stop at nothing to take care of them and protect them.

Even in those difficult years, I kept my work discipline strong. Never did I abandon my goal to be Store Director. I knew that was the way out. I knew that achieving that goal would change the course of my life forever, and that I would break a vicious cycle for the better benefit of my family. Failure wasn't an option. Through all my mental suffering, I never called out sick and I continued to give 110% effort to work every day. This was for my kids and I was going to win this one for US!

By this time, I was an assistant store manager, meaning that I was just one step away from my goal. I made more money now than I had made in my whole life, so I knew that I was getting closer...closer to my dream of becoming 100% legitimate.

Decision Time...

On the first day of that summer in Montebello, a boy was shot and died in the apartments where we were living, and no more than two weeks later, one of the main shot callers from the South Side Montebello Gang was murdered right in front of our apartments, right next to where I parked my car. He was gunned down just minutes after I had seen him standing in his front yard flashing his guns to all of his fellow gang members.

By this time, my twin brothers were about eleven years old and my sister was already sixteen.

My two kids were about five and eight years of age. I had taken them when I finally left my ex-wife and now they were living with me. The day that I left Heather for good my son, Cody, was about four years old. I grabbed my laundry basket with all my clothes and proceeded to leave. I knew that this relationship between Heather and I was over and that I would not be coming back to live ever again. That night Cody also grabbed his laundry basket with his clothes in it and chased me out of the door. He yelled, "Dad, where ever you go I am going too!" I cry as I type because I can still feel the pain as I was exiting. I felt so alone as I walked to my car and my little son refused to stay behind. His happy place was with his father. It just goes to show that your kids are always watching the show of your life. At four years old, Cody had pledged his loyalty to his father, and to this very day he and I still have this bond that is absolutely magical. Unbreakable.

I have NEVER been without my kids. When my ex-wife and I split up, I gladly took the kids with me. I knew that I could give them a better life because I saw that she didn't give a fuck about anyone but herself anymore. If she was going downhill in life, I refused to let my kids go down, too. Ashley and Cody were way too valuable for me to just let go and give up. I would fight to the death for my children. Their safety and overall well-being was my top priority in life. I was determined to give my kids a better life and would stop at nothing to make this happen.

So, after that second murder in Montebello, I said "Fuck this place! We are leaving here!" I went to Costa Mesa and, with no hesitation, dropped three thousand for us to move in to the Villa Sienna Apartments (formerly known as "Our Town Apartments"). That very weekend my mom, my siblings, and my kids loaded up the moving truck and all ten of us moved in to a three-bedroom, two-bath apartment in Costa Mesa. We had all finally made it back to CM!!

I felt really good about this move, and I still do, to this day. That move made it possible for my twin brothers Dan and Ray to have a fair shot in life. It also made it possible for my little sister to finish high school and graduate from the same school that I graduated from. From this point moving forward, I began to coast through life and for the moment it wasn't so bad anymore.

These summers were some of the best days of my life with my kids, my brothers and sister, my mom, Jesse, and Mikey, my sister's boyfriend and father of her two children. We were all together, and we just made it work. We were all safe. Most importantly, the kids would have a safe place to live and have a fair shot at life.

We now had new apartment for all of us and I had a new job. I had had to step down from the assistant store manager position to be a department manager so that I could take care of my kids during the night. I was totally exhausted from working 60+ hours a week and commuting to and from Montebello every day. Life was still tough. My life was all about the grind whether I liked it, or not.

But now at this time depression had set in like a motherfucker.

I used to drink myself to sleep and cry in the silence of my heart over my family. I had loved my ex-wife with all of my heart and I could not believe she fucked us over the way she did. I mean she totally checked out on us. She went full blown party girl, started hanging out with hoodlums, refused to mother her kids, and always had a reason to not come and see them. On top of all of that, because Cody was extremely loyal to his father, she did not want to have anything to do with him. Emotionally, I was an absolute mess. I felt as if I was stuck in a bad place and had no way out. I had learned to master the art of not showing pain and putting on a smile for all to see. I never wanted to be seen as soft or weak, but clearly at this point in my life my heart was broken...again. **But no matter what, I still had to carry on for my kids.**

Chapter 26: New Job=Haters

I got a new job at Bristol Farms in Mission Viejo California. At the new job, some of the old timers were hating on me big time! Everyone there was jealous as fuck that I got hired in as a manager with good pay. I wasn't used to everyone in the workplace hating me, so this was a very big adjustment. A group of nasty females even set me up and tried to get me fired on some bullshit. I signed a final warning on some shit that I didn't even do. Clearly a few rotten apples were out to get me. I had to deal with it, though. I was a single dad raising two kids on my own and needed that job to stay afloat.

Life was still fucked for me as I was struggling with depression and just trying to pick up the pieces. They made us take one-hour lunches daily, which really sucked because any down time for me would result in me just thinking about my ex-wife and family. I still had to be strong and carry on for my kids.

After about a year I was transferred to Bristol Farms in Newport Beach, California. I was happy to work so close to home; I was almost in my own backyard. There was a team full of all stars at that location. Newport Beach and Beverly Hills were the two super powers of that company. I was excited to play on the dream team, and I loved the environment. There were lots of wealthy clientele and a whole lot of good looking women in that demographic! It was a good time for me as I was learning to live again. I was starting to have fun and enjoy life again. I was really focused in the area of "learning to forgive" as my anger had brought me to my knees. I did not want to be hateful anymore. I wanted to be what I called NORMAL again. I wanted to be that guy with a great personality that everyone gravitated towards again. When I took on that challenge of "forgiveness," the doors of life opened again for James Merrifield!

True story.

One Sunday evening I went grocery shopping for the week. Kids would be back in school on Monday so it was time to load up the fridge. My depression and anger were really eating me alive at the time and I was really starting to go insane. As I was standing in line to pay for my groceries I was in a deep stare when I realized that I was staring at the book and magazine racks located at the check stand. Once my vision came in to focus I was staring a book that was written by Dr.Phil. The title of the book was something like "10 ways to improve your life". So I figured what the heck? My life was already in the toilette, what could this book possibly do for me? Well, without hesitation I bought it. There were several chapters based on self-improvement but the one area that stood out the most was the chapter about learning to forgive. I struggled with forgiveness my entire life. If you lived my life you would understand my pain. You would fully know why when I developed a grudge it stained my mind and heart at full capacity. But like I said in the previous paragraph that once I committed to forgiving Heather for destroying our family I was able to live in peace for the first time in my life.

Very shortly after this encounter my ex-wife had really hit rock bottom. I told her when she left me/us that she was making a huge mistake. Like a smart ass who thought she was in full control of her life, she said to me in the most sarcastic tone, "Well, I guess I will have to learn on my own now won't I, James?" Those were the words that had now bitten her right in her ass!

I had to step in and help her. Even though she screwed me and the kids over, it wasn't all about me. It was about my kids. For those of you men who have been through a crappy divorce, you all know that the mother's attitude greatly affects the children, and I did not want that negative energy migrating into my home. Sometimes you must bite the bullet and take it like a man. That is exactly what I did. My ex-wife was fired from her little bullshit apartment manager job and had nowhere to live, so I dropped a down payment to get her an apartment. She also was six months late on her car payment and lost her car, so I cosigned to get her a new car. I know...I know...I'm was an idiot, right? No, I wasn't! My career in the grocery business was about to take full flight and I did not need anything standing in my way. I wasn't doing this for my ex-wife; I was doing this for the mother of my children. I did it so that when my kids went to visit her, they would have a place to stay and when she needed transportation to come and get them, she would have a vehicle to do it with. There is always a bigger picture. My kids had suffered enough, and I was doing my best to help stop the bleeding. Whether you like it or not, there will be a time in your life that you will have to be the bigger man. Whether I liked it or not...it was my turn to be that person.

Chapter 27: Veronica

September of 2007 rolled around. This was the year that one of my biggest blessings came in to my life as I met the woman who would be the biggest difference maker in the life of me and my children.

After almost three years at Bristol Farms, my first mentor called me to come on board with what is now one of the largest natural food grocery retail businesses in the U.S. At the time that I accepted the offer they only had four stores in California. Ten years later, we have over 300 locations nationwide. I never expected this company to grow the way that it did, but life has an interesting way of just making things happen.

About three months before I left Bristol Farms to move on to bigger and better things, I met Veronica. This part of the story is very interesting because you never know who you are standing next to. You could be standing next to a millionaire and not know it. You could be looking eye to eye with a stone-cold killer and not know it. One day as I was walking to the back receiving area of the store, Veronica was standing next to the entry way and I stopped to say hello to her and a mutual friend. I was literally saying hello to the woman who would be my new wife.

Now I must admit that at very first, I was not in to her at all, though she will tell you a different story. Really, she was a nice girl with a big smile. She tried to get me to take her to go see a movie. I think the movie was *The Transformers*. I denied her, softly saying that I was going to go watch the movie with my kids. Later she also asked me out on another date, and I cancelled out at the last minute by text message, which to this day she swears that she never got.

It is so very strange because, during my last week of employment with Bristol Farms, I knew that baseball season was quickly coming to an end and I had been wanting to go see one last Dodger game. Just two days before I was slated to leave Bristol Farms, Veronica approached me and asked if I would be interested in going to a Dodger Game with her. She said she had an extra seat in the boxes behind third base, and because I am a huge Dodger fan, I could not resist, so I agreed to go with her.

The day of the Dodger game was as awkward as they come. I was running very late pick Veronica up and, considering that I actually dodged her for two dates prior, I was now feeling like a jerk. That day my son Cody did what he is most famous for. He tells me at very last minute that he needed a big red poster board and some other art supplies for a school project, so I was in

California traffic running around last minute at three p.m. on a Thursday to locate these items! I went to four different locations to get everything that he needed! At almost six p.m. I FINALLY I made it to her house in Buena Park California. When I got to the house, I called her to say, "Let's go!" Veronica stayed quiet for a second and then she said, "My dad wants to meet you." In my most sarcastic tone, I said to myself, *Fuck!* For the last three years I had been used to messing around with older, faster women. This was a first for me, but out of respect for this young lady, I went up to the door and gently knocked. In just a moment, I met the man who would be not only my future father-in-law but one of the best examples ever of a husband role model. Danny was very kind and had a big smile on his face. We shook hands and then I told him that I was in a hurry to get back on the freeway.

Veronica and I jumped in my truck and sped off in to L.A. Before the game, I took Veronica to my favorite restaurant in L.A. called Paul's Cantonese Kitchen, right there in downtown. After dinner, I drove down the side streets, passing through skid row and into China Town. By the time we hit the back side of the Chavez Ravine (Dodger Stadium), I could tell that she was really into me. Driving two miles per hour, waiting in line to get into Dodger Stadium, I was really enjoying my buzz. The very moment when I thought that things could not get any better, Veronica placed her hand on top of mine. I gotta give her an A+ for being so persistent! That night, our first kiss was in the beer line at Dodger Stadium and the two of us have been together since that moment. We really are a true story of what team work in a relationship is really all about. Are we perfect? Fuck no! By all means, we do have our faults and differences, but one thing is for sure. We always come to a compromise and we always make decisions that will benefit the entire family. We both remain dedicated to the PURPOSE of LOVE and FAMILY. That is our secret to our successful marriage and relationship. We work on it daily.

At the age of twenty-three, Veronica immediately jumped in there with both feet and mothered my two children as if they were her very own. It was like she was a professional parent who just knew what was needed and knew what to do. She came from an extremely well-structured home—the complete opposite of my upbringing. Josie and Danny (my in-laws) did a great job raising Veronica as she is a true instrument of LOVE and DEVOTION to her family.

All I ever knew in life was to work hard and hope that everything would fall in to place. Veronica made all the difference in our home. She was the missing piece to my life's puzzle. I finally found what I had been praying for and more. When Heather and I parted ways for the second time, I had created a mental list of what I needed in the next woman who would come into my life. The first thing on that list and, most important to me, was that she had to have God in her heart. This was the biggest necessity that I had to have. The second thing was that she had to be 100% dedicated to her family, just as I was to mine. And third, I did not need anything, ANYTHING else in this life but to just be loved and accepted for the person that I was. Nothing more and nothing less. The search was over; I had found what I had been looking for.

In the meantime, my future mother and father-in-law were not too happy with the idea of me being in the picture. Their concerns were that I had been married once before and had two kids. They gave Veronica a lot of grief over us being a couple. She would call me or come to my apartment with tears in her eyes and tell me that her mom and dad did not want her to see me anymore. I had difficulty accepting this and would seek wise counsel from the few mentors that were in my life. I pleaded my case before them and the advice that I received was great! I was told that I was not a good guy, but that I was a great fucking guy and that I did not need to do anything more than just be myself! Imagine that!! Just be myself!! Now why on earth didn't I think of that?! I suppose that I knew that all along. I guess I really had difficulties with not being accepted, but because I loved Veronica so much, there was no way in hell that I would just walk away from our relationship due to a few parental concerns. I knew in my heart that I was going to marry this woman and it would be me and her against the world!

I knew that I would be getting promoted to store director very soon (finally!!!) and my plan was to build my family with Veronica fully in the picture. She and I had planned to move in together......unmarried. Veronica told me that her parents were going to flip out on her. You see, my wife's side of the family is hard-core Catholic and moving in together and having sex and all of that before marriage is hard-core prohibited.

The day came when Veronica told her parents that she would be moving in with me. My mother and father-in-law stood their ground and told my wife that if we did this that they would not accept me and that we would not be welcome in their home. My wife is a very sensitive, caring, and loving individual, so of course she was deeply wounded by this.

So Big Chunk did exactly what he felt was necessary. I told them that I was going to marry their daughter that week. The response was epic!! "Hold on!! Wait!! It doesn't have to happen so soon!!..." But I wasn't asking for permission. I was going to marry that girl. I told them that we were going to the courthouse on July 3 and that she would be going to be my wife. Veronica would come home for the parties, the holidays, birthdays, and even come visit on the weekends. But on that day, I made it clear that she was coming with me. She did, and we were married.

When you believe in something big enough with all your heart and soul you must do it. That is where you will find your true calling in life. That is where your peace of mind and soul. Your parents will guide you through your life the best that they can but just remember that the LIFE JOURNEY belongs to YOU. At the end of the day you as the individual must decide what is going to best suit you. And most important you have to own your decisions 110%. Win or lose, you own it.

My love for Veronica was so enormous that I knew that I was going to spend the rest of my life with her. She had the one and only thing that I needed in this world, that ONE THING that would make my life complete, her unconditional LOVE.

To this day I tell Veronica that the only thing that I need from her in life is her LOVE. This is true. We have our differences, as all couples do, but at the end of the day our entire foundation is based on LOVE.

I was just dairy manager when we met at Bristol Farms in Newport Beach California. Ten years later I am a Store

Director for one of the largest retailers of natural foods in the U.S. and I am also the President and CEO of our own Company (ACJ Investment Company). Veronica believed in me like no one else ever did. She believed in me ten years ago when I first shared my goals with her and continues to believe in me when I present her with new goals....MUCH BIGGER GOALS.

She has given me another son, James Daniel Merrifield, who has brought more joy in to my life than I could have ever dreamt possible. We own a home in Costa Mesa California and have successfully raised our two older children, Ashley and Cody, together. In my book of life, this is SUCCESS and just goes to show that ANYTHING that you set your mind to do can and will be done.

I once made a comment that my children have everything that I ever wanted when I was a kid. They have a great life and a solid family foundation. Someone very graciously replied "But now look at you James. Now you have everything that you have ever wanted". This is true tenfold. It takes a lot of love and dedication to raise a family, and to create that legacy that will last for an eternity.

The next ten years would fly by faster than any other decade in all my life. So please pay close attention.

Chapter 28: The Rolling 30s

NOW FROM THIS POINT ON, I REALLY NEED YOU TO STAY CLOSE TO ME.   YOU ALREADY READ ABOUT MY YOUNG LIFE AND PART OF MY ADULTHOOD.   NOW IT'S TIME FOR ME TO EMBRACE GROWING UP, FACING NEW CHALLENGES, AND FOCUSING ON FULLY MATURING.   THE STORY ONLY GETS MORE INTERESTING.

At thirty years of age I had a lot going on…..

Question: Who gets a huge promotion, gets married on July 3, parties like a rock star with my new wife over the 4th of July weekend, moves all of our shit into our new apartment on Back Bay, AND starts at his new store location as a newly promoted Store Director on Monday?????? You guessed it! #ME!!

So, now that everything was situated, and my life is going in the right direction, I was feeling very comfortable and very content. Life was just booming with success and I was just flowing in the right direction. However, when you feel like a champ and think that life is just so wonderful that you can now live life on cruise control…you better think again. This is the time where you need to be able to assess what is going on all around you because no matter how good life can be, there will always be a new challenge waiting for you. Whether you like it or not, a new season awaits you. In this next chapter you will learn about the seasons of life. Seasons come and go. If you are enduring hard times, you must not worry, for a new season will begin and the hard times will be gone. This is part of the learning process. Hang in there.

At the age of thirty, my health was starting to go to shit. I was diagnosed with type 2 diabetes in 2009 and, I was having a really hard time managing this disease. It was all so brand new to me. As a matter of fact, the disease was managing me. From 2009 to 2011, I was hospitalized twice. At the time I was diagnosed, I weighed 331 pounds. I knew that I had to make some drastic changes in my health regime, so I began to educate myself in the area of health and wellness. If you really want to make the best changes that are suited for ANY AREA of your life, you MUST take it upon yourself to do your own research. Doctors with degrees are killing people in America with their drug prescriptions and malpractice, so you need to be very careful with the prescription drugs that you are taking. Band aids will never stop the bleeding, but it will allow you to bleed to death very slowly if you do not keep a close eye on it.

These so-called doctors wanted to pump me up with every drug in the world. When I told them that I was not feeling the same, the response that I got was epic. I was told that that it was all in my head. I told that doctor to "go to hell" and that's when I knew that if I did not seek further help, I would be another victim of these so-called doctors and type 2 diabetes.

In a situation like this what does one do?

I went out and found myself a real holistic practitioner, who to this day I am very close to. I give full credit to helping me get my health back in order. John Robbins is his name. He is the CEO of ANT Nutrition. John is by far one of the most intelligent and most caring individuals that I have ever met, and I still call him friend. This man is by far more knowledgeable than any doctor that I have ever met and is deeply affiliated with men like Dr. Yoshiaki Omura and Dr. Bob Marshall. These men are extremely intelligent human beings who are part of a society that has been known to cure cancer in the human body permanently through natural earthly practices. It is because of John that I believe that the human body can cure itself. With the right guidance, health can be very optimal for those who truly seek it. Just know that you will have to do your own due diligence as much research will be required to make such drastic changes. Today I am all the down from 331 pounds to 240 pounds and I feel great. I take a few supplements to assist with healthy living, such as digestive enzymes for proper nutrient absorption, hydrochloric acid to ensure that my food is distributed to the proper channels, and psyllium husk to ensure that my digestive track is properly functioning. All these supplements work together to help me stay lean and fit. I go to the gym four to five days a week and do a combination of cardiovascular workouts, weight training workouts, and hard-core abdominal workouts. I like to change up the work outs about every two months to keep things fresh and stay motivated. After my workouts, I will have an all organic vegan protein shake that is loaded with probiotics and green vegetables. My eating habits have totally changed and so has my lifestyle. I believe that YOU MUST embrace some sort of physical activity for thirty minutes to one hour daily. The heart is the strongest muscle in your body, so you must take care of it and treat it as if it were the most important organ in your body…because it is.

In 2010, I stopped partying. Cold Turkey. <u>ONCE AGAIN you can do anything that you set your mind to do. No excuses.</u>

My employer established a policy stating that anyone who got hurt on the job or had any kind of incident involving the paramedics or hospitalization of any kind would result in the employee having to do a mandatory drug test. With my health going south, I knew that a little weed smoke was not worth me getting fired and losing a hundred thousand a year. I had worked way too hard to get to this point in my life and just like that, I stopped getting high. Ever since that day I have never looked back. If anything, I felt ashamed to think that I wasted many years of my life, my time, and so much money to support that kind of habit. It is truly amazing to see how much more money is in your bank account when you leave old expensive habits in the dust. I had to grow up now and be smarter than I had ever been before. Many new challenges were standing before me and if you know like I know, when it's sink or swim; you've got to think to win.

On top of that, there were lots of politics in the workplace. This was another adjustment that I needed to make. I could no longer go around punking people like a street thug. As most of you know, if you rub the wrong person the wrong way that could get you black balled from an entire industry or fired in an instant. Lucky for me, I was in good standing with the men who were running the company, so I really took advantage of the examples that were set before me. If you want to be the best in any field, you must learn from the best and practice being the very best. Competition and the struggle for company supremacy was very real. Being

James Merrifield I was extremely street fight competitive for results. I had to be #1 at anything that we did. From sales to bottom line contribution dollars there was a time when I gave this company the best profit and loss statements that they had ever seen in California.

For the last ten years, I had been fortunate enough to be close to our Western Divisional Vice-President, as well as his protégé—who just happened to be my mentor for over twenty years. I learned lots of tough lessons. Some lessons fell in my favor and others did not, but during those ten years, I would build a solid foundation on rock-solid ground and would not only earn the respect of the elders but would also be recognized as one of the absolute top performers in our entire company. In ten years I am the only person to receive TWO Store Manager of The Year Awards from this company. Both of those awards reside in the trash. I NEVER went to work and showed up with an intent to work for an award. I do things the way I do because it is the RIGHT THING to do. They call me The Coach because I'm 110% for real. Any team that I coached became known for dominating their competition. I was determined to make winners out of everyone, and I was recognized for that on several occasions. I was also given several awards from The Supreme Court for helping those with a troubled past get their lives back in order. I helped women who had gotten their kids taken away by the state get those kids back and taught them how to manage a department and also manage their lives. I helped felons who did a minimum of five years prison time, become full blown responsible individuals. One of those individual is now a dedicated family man and runs a 15 million dollar a year operation in Nevada. Another individual makes close to 60k a year and is a dedicated family man who teaches his kids how to play soccer on the weekends.

I pride myself on winning and I make people around me better, whether they like it or not. This is a disease that I developed as a child because I always felt like we were a joke. Now more than ever, I was on a mission to build an empire. I was truly able to motivate, teach, and successfully coach people by the masses to do the right thing. I was passing down my twenty plus years of knowledge DAILY because I am a very firm believer in the theory that we are ONLY as strong as our WEAKEST link. Success before death, No one on my team fails.

In 2010 I gave SFM the best profit and loss reports that they had ever seen in the California West Division, and I won a Store of the Year award. That year, my wife and I were flown up to our corporate headquarters in Arizona and were housed at some fancy resort in Scottsdale.

I remember when I got off the plane and into my rental car, I turned on the radio.

Instantaneously, the song "Juicy" by Biggie Smalls came on.

The song began to play and I cranked up the volume. The lyrics began and it said: "It was all a dream!!!"

James Merrifield had finally made it!! Not only did I achieve my goal of being a Store Director, but with street fight competitive mentality and a heart of gold, I had seen my dream become my reality! I was 110% legitimate. I was able to walk completely away from the stupid shit that I had done, and I could finally live the normal life that I had always wanted.

The day I received a Store of the Year Award, my first mentor was present, which was very special to me. As the CEO was announcing my name he was yelling at me to get my ass up and get on stage. He was so proud of me. I was proud of me. Had this man not been in my corner for the last twenty years, I would not be where I am today. No doubt, I had to work my ass off to get to where I am today, but without his influence and his example, there would be no James Merrifield in the grocery industry. He was like the influential "dad" that I never had in my life. He was very harsh and very demanding, but he always meant well. On the night of the ceremony, my wife Veronica was present by my side, and our Vice President of The California West Division, as well. This man would also play a major role in my life. He was extremely classy and taught both me and my mentor how to behave both on and off of the field. I am forever grateful for him hiring me and trusting me with his millions of dollars. He gave me a chance to shine at what I felt I was most good at, and I know that he too was most proud of me.

This was a major accomplishment for me.

From the kid who lived a tough young life, and had several setbacks as a young adult, to a thirty-three-year old man doing it real big, I proved to myself that I could do ANYTHING that I set my mind to do. I had truly amazed myself, and I know that I shocked the shit out of anyone who had known me since I was a youngster. If you knew me from day one, you would have never guessed that I would have made it this far.

Every time I would venture back to the old hood of East L.A. or Pico Rivera for some sort of reunion (which the majority of the time was a funeral) I found it very odd that people were now avoiding me. I would attend these events with my mother. I would ask her why people were acting so strange around me. Her was response was that they are very intimidated by you James. I never go back to the hood with a goodie good mentality because I came from there and I know what the day to day grind feels like. I NEVR forgot where I came from. Sometimes when attending a Chamber of Commerce meeting in Newport Beach or Playing Golf at a Charity Tournament at the Elegant Pelican Hill, I still feel different. I still feel like Im a part of a different breed. And don't get me wrong…during these times I am 110% authentic me. And for whatever reason, I am totally the life of the party. Im that guy that people want to get to know.

On the flip side, to this day, some will tell me now that I was always special and that they knew that I would make it. I just smile. In my mind I can't help but to think *B.S.* These were some of the same people who put me down as a kid and always had something negative to say.

When you are truly on a mission, don't be afraid to put the horse blinders on to stay focused. When others do not understand your mission and cannot relate to your passion, they will be full of comments and opinions that will only distract you from pursuing your dreams. I had a goal and a tremendous amount of FAITH and knew that someday I was going to be someone. I was going to go places that no one else in my family had ever gone. My life goal was to break a vicious cycle and that's exactly what I did.

I have found that when you are completely misunderstood by the masses, this means that you my friend are a leader. The majority sheep cannot comprehend the mindset of a man with a vision and a definitive purpose. And remember its not your job to persuade the entire world to work for greatness, though you can try. People have to want greatness. People have to be willing to pay the price for it, <u>and pay it gladly.</u>

Chapter 29: My Kids

Even with all the effort that I put into my work life, I still made it a point to work twice as hard on my family life. Veronica and the kids would have my complete attention, and no matter what, I would not allow the family foundation to be second place in my life.

I cannot help but think of how many precious memories my dad missed out on because he wasn't around. I cannot help but think of how many other fathers out there miss out on the best things in life such as a child's sporting events, award ceremonies, school activities, family events, or just time at the dinner table together.

Some that read this will say, "James Merrifield, you don't understand the hustle. You don't understand what is going on with my life." "I'm Busy" Blah, blah, blah, blah.

In no uncertain terms, please allow me to clarify for you exactly what the "hustle" means.

Not only did I raise two kids alone at a very delicate time of their young lives, but I also worked five days a week, eleven hours a day, and drove forty-five miles one way from OC to LA for work. On top of that, I showed up on the football field at 6:30 p.m. during the week days to coach Cody and his team until 8:30 p.m., took both kids home for showers, fed them dinner, did home work, and put them to bed. I did this daily. This was my life for several years! Oh, and by the way, game day was on Saturday. Yes, every Saturday from the time Cody was seven until he went to high school, I was on that field doing what I loved to do.

Do not ever allow yourself to make excuses as to why you cannot be involved in your kids' lives. Your kids need you more than you will ever know. Stay committed and, no matter what, stay engaged.

It is said that at a certain age, that is when your kids need you the most. I disagree with all of that. Raising a family is a process. Your kids need you to be in the picture their entire life. Their entire life depends on you being there for them through thick and thin. There are no such things as a parental off day or a parental vacation. This job is a life sentence with some of the absolute most rewarding times that you will get to experience in your entire life.

You can do whatever you set your mind to do. At this stage of my life, I was training my own mind to be selfless and put others' needs before my own. My life wasn't about me then, and it is still not about me. It never was about me! It is and will always be about my family, my friends, my Team Members (employees), and my community. My life is about doing my ABSOLUTE best to be the ABSOLUTE biggest difference maker in as many lives as I can possibly be!

I am just the guy who gets to drive the bus. But for me, clearly it's all about the people that are my passengers.

Starting in 2007, I was blessed to be a part of my son, Cody's, football team staff. Our time together only served to strengthen the body between us. So many special memories took place on those football fields. It was more than just winning. (Though winning does make it more fun!) It was about the relationships that were built between those kids and me. It was about the relationships that were built with their parents. To this day, there are several of us parents who keep in contact and, of course, our kids still support each other and have each other's backs. Some of these kids went on to play Division 1 football in high school and every year I put some money aside in my budget to help pay for some of those tuitions. I do this out of love. If you are in position to help others, you must do so. This is part of life. Giving out of the kindness of your heart and expecting nothing in return speaks volumes about who you really are. Don't misunderstand. I am not filthy rich. I just believe in doing the right thing, for the right cause.

My daughter, Ashley was my first inspiration. Having a daughter at eighteen years old can really change your perspective of women. I would do anything in my power to protect her because I am very well aware that there are some dirt bag men out there. I will be damned if any man should ever think that he was going to spit on my hard work and put shame on our last name. Both Veronica and I were very tough on Ashley because we intended to create a strong young lady who would never have to be at the mercy of any man, or any person for that matter. We were setting her up for greatness, and we are extremely proud of her and her accomplishments.

Ashley was on the cheer squad, and our back-bone, Veronica, made sure that my kids made it to practice every day on time. I would show up at the park right at 6 p.m. when practice got started. Like I said, this was our life. My son Cody would go on to play tackle football for ten years. By the time Cody turned seventeen, he had started in well over one hundred tackle football games. He was given several Scholar Athlete Awards and All Conference Honors.

But I was the lucky one. Out of those ten years, I only missed one football game. I prided myself on being there for my children. Out of numerous award ceremonies between both of my two older children, I do believe that I did not miss one event! Being a Super Dad came so natural for me because I wanted to be involved in EVERYTHING! I have built my life around my family. I have sacrificed my life to ensure that they had whatever they needed. Their joy is my priority. Their happiness means everything to me.

Parents who truly love their children will always find a way to make the most important things in life happen for them. Others will make excuses. Keep in mind that your hard work and dedication will be their hard work and dedication when they get older. So always lead by example; they are always watching you.

On October 24, 2012, I was given a brand-new blessing. My son, James Daniel Merrifield, was born. I must admit that I was a little scared of being a dad again. I had already fought many battles in my youth, and now I would be going to battle one more time, for the last time. My son, Cody, had just turned twelve and Ashley was fifteen. (Yes, I know that's a big age gap!) However, part of Veronicas dream was to have a child of her own, and it was only right that I made the love of my life's dream come true. She supported my kids and me since day one with zero hesitations and no limitations. Veronica would now be in for the time of her life.

Raising kids is some very serious business. At least to me it is. There are no days off. There is no rest break. There are no sick days and there is no mercy. Every day is a playoff game in the world of parenting. My new son, James Daniel, brought so much joy to our home. He was nothing at all like my first two children. As a baby, this kid was very wild and was always crying and fussing if he was not being held. For the first three months, he was just sucking the life out of me!! LMAO!

I guess he just wanted to be loved right? Well, who doesn't?

Fast forward to today. He is the most loving kid on the planet whose biggest desire is to follow in his big brother's footsteps. I just want to do everything with him that I did with Ashley and Cody. My Uncle Greg told me when I was much younger that the best times that you will ever have with your children are the times that required you to spend absolutely NO MONEY. I have found this to be true. I have memories of summer time, in the pool with Ashley, that are embedded in my mind for life. Teaching my three kids to swim was so magical. The day those floaties came off was a big milestone for the kids and for me. I have memories of playing at Shiffer Park with my kids that will stay in my mind forever. We would spend hours playing on the slides, the swings and, the monkey bars. During these trips there was NO MONEY SPENT. IT WAS ALL ABOUT LOVE AND QUALITY TIME. Someday when I leave this earth, my kids will also have those priceless memories to hold on to forever. <u>LOVE IS FREE.</u> <u>THE ABSOLUTE BEST THING IN LIFE IS FREE!!</u>

As with my first two kids, I took James Daniel (JD) EVERYWHERE—the parks, the beaches, the little road trips, sometime even just for a ride to the grocery store. He's even been to Cabo San Lucas and the Bahamas! He is now my new project. My little buddy. My Pal.

Just the other day as I scrolled through my Instagram (IG) history, I was once again reminded of what a devoted father I am. All my pictures are either of my kids or inspirational quotes. *That history really motivates me because a great father is all that I ever wanted to be.* All I ever wanted to be was the best provider for my family that I could possibly be. Nothing in this world means more to me than my family. NOTHING!! I would do anything for them before myself.

Sometimes we all need reminders of how far we have come. I know I do. I am my very own worst critic. I am harder on myself than anyone else could possibly ever be! Growing up with nothing and a heart full of scars was enough motivation for me to be one of the biggest success stories of my time. Before the age of ten, I saw it all. I saw exactly what I wanted in life and knew what to stay away from. It was like the road map to my success, my blueprint, was already being put together right before my eyes and I was already being prepped for my life's journey. Did I make some mistakes? Absolutely! Did I learn from those mistakes? Yes, I did! But the point that

I am trying to make here is that all I ever wanted to have in life is exactly what I have strived to give to my children.

In summer of 2013, Ashley graduated from Newport Harbor High School. The thought of having an eighteen-year-old graduate kind of freaked me out. I thought to myself *"You're getting old James"* But the fact that I had Cody and JD still at home was my security blanket. My life still had some deep purpose to it. However, this was the start of a few chains of events that would change my life again forever.

My daughter was now growing into a woman. As parents, all we can do is our very best and HOPE that our kids will carry on as responsible adults. Please trust me when I say that our house was like boot camp for raising kids. Veronica and I felt that, if we were going to work our asses off as parents, then we would demand that our children would also understand the need to be their very best as well. We would not settle for anything less than a great effort, and a job well done.

Chapter 30: Death Again

In July of 2014, my mom's boyfriend of sixteen years, Jessie, died. Jesse had been diagnosed with stage four cancer out of nowhere, and it took him down fast. This was very sad for me because, at the time, Jesse and my mom were not on good terms at all. I know that this saddened my twin brothers, Dan and Ray, along with my sister, Christina. It just wasn't right. The timing wasn't right. The timing for this kind of stuff is never right. I wasn't ready to say goodbye to Jesse just yet. The day that I found out about Jesse's cancer, I had a business meeting in Cerritos. As soon as that meeting was over, I raced to Montebello where he was staying with his niece to see how he was doing. When I arrived, he was just posted up in the bed room like a patient in a hospital, but the second he heard my voice, he jumped to his feet, so excited to see me. I will never forget the hug that he gave me. It was almost as if he was already saying goodbye. I asked him WTF was going on and then he started to tell me the story about how he found out that he was dying from cancer. I just sat on the bed and gave him my full attention until he was done speaking. That day when we said our goodbyes, I told him that I would return soon, and that there were some good products that I knew of that could help with his health. No, I am not a doctor, but my first instinct was to help. I wanted to see

Jesse beat this. I kept telling myself that he was going to be okay. I didn't want to see him leave this earth so soon. This man was good to my mother and my twin brothers and sister. Jesse had my back too. When my ex-wife Heather turned her back on me and kicked me out, Jesse had welcomed me in to their two-bedroom apartment in Montebello with zero hesitation. I lived in two-bedroom apartments almost my entire life. Some of the best moments of my life took place in those apartments. They were so small, and even though we were stacked on top of each other in very close quarters, we always made it work and we always had enough. The small space actually kept us very close to one another.

A week later I went back to Montebello, and he looked very tired and weak. I could see that the cancer was now in full effect, and there would be no miracle of mercy on his life expectancy. About a month later, in July, Jesse finally passed away. When I received the news, I was tending to my little garden on our back patio. I immediately drove to the 7-11 liquor store and bought a three pack of Bud Light tall cans and poured some in the dirt for Jesse. He had loved the Bud Light Tall cans. He also loved his mixed nuts and beef jerky. These are the things that remind me of Jesse. He was always so generous with whatever he had. He would give the shirt off his back if you needed it. My friend was gone. This was very sudden for me and hard to accept.

To make matters worse, my mother was not welcome at his funeral. His nieces told me that my brothers and sisters were allowed to come, but if my mom showed up, they would ask her to leave. I showed up that night and jumped on stage to give him one of the greatest farewell speeches that anyone could have ever been given. I respected that man to a T. I loved him and had a significant amount of respect for him. The bottom line is that he took my brothers and sisters in as his very own children and provided for them until the day he passed. THAT'S A REAL MAN IN MY BOOK!! Rest in Love, Jesse Martinez. You will never be forgotten. You will always have a place in my heart.

About a month after Jesse left this earth, my daughter Ashley broke the news to me that she would be moving out of our house. I didn't expect it. I never saw it coming.

It was a warm summer night, and I had bar-b-qued for my family. I do this every Sunday. I love to cook, listen to music, have a few beers, and smoke a good cigar. Veronica and I like to go to bed early on Sundays as work comes very fast on a Monday. Normally everything is cleaned up by 6 p.m. and we are racing to lie in bed and relax.

That day I woke up around 9 p.m. feeling a bit dehydrated. I needed a glass of water. As I came downstairs, Ashley must have heard my big footsteps. Ashley stood there in the dark with tears running down her face and said that she needed to talk to me. Instantly, I thought, *Oh God, She's pregnant!!* But it wasn't that. Not even close. She began to tell me that she wanted to move out on her own. She said that she was crying because she didn't want me to be mad at her or hate her for leaving. I told her that if she walked out that door that she would need a good game plan because this world is very cruel and can be extremely demanding. She said that she wanted to take a shot at life on her own. I had no choice but to accept her will.

That night it was as if I had gotten hit with a left hook to the jaw. Bam!! Punch landed!! When your kids are eighteen, they have the freedom to do what they want because they are now adults. She packed up all her personal belongings, and the very next day Ashley was gone.

I worried a lot for the next three months. Ashley had lived under the safety of my roof her entire life and anyone who truly knows me knows that I will fight to the death to protect and preserve the lives of my wife and children. Ashley remains in my prayers. Before I go to sleep, I ask God to please ensure her safety and to help her know that if she needs anything from us, we are here to help. Letting go of your kids is not the easiest thing to do. Yeah, the letting go thing is brutal on the heart, especially when you have dedicated your life to your kids. The truth is that over the past twenty years I had done a lot of planning and prepping for my life, but letting go of my kids was not on that list.

Chapter 31: My Dad Dies

A few months later, we bought our first house in Costa Mesa. I was very excited. I never thought that I would be a home owner. This was a big first step for me, but most definitely not the biggest. People always told me that buying a home was one of the biggest moves in life that I would ever make. That's bullshit. I can think of MANY other things that are way more important that buying a home. Don't get me wrong. I am blessed to own a home. It's just not the biggest blessing.

In my new home there were both big and small opportunities as far as fixing things up and I really had hoped that maybe this would be my chance to bond with my dad. I really needed this closure in my life. I knew that my dad had cirrhosis of the liver and was not in good shape, but I figured that he could come over and coach me up on how to do the repairs because he was incredibly talented in the area of construction, plumbing, electrical, concrete, etc.

See, even though I've been to hundreds of baseball games with my wife and kids, I never went to one baseball game with my dad. I've had many good times partying it up with my wife and two older kids, but I never had a beer with my dad. No fishing trips with dad, no football games with dad...nothing. What I'm trying to say is that I really wanted some closure, but once again I would get fucked out of the deal.

Life wasn't done thrashing my emotions around. The season was long and painful.

My dad's cirrhosis got worse and worse. The sad thing about it is that the woman who he left me for and all of her kids went "hands-off" when he got extremely ill. I did not understand this move at all and I wasn't trying to either. I thought *How in the fuck do you go hands-off when you have known him your whole lives?!! For God's sake, your kids called him grandpa! He didn't even know my kids' birthdays, or even my birthday. He was there for all of you and your kids, but you went cold on him like that?!*

The best part is that my not-so-smart aunt, who was in charge of my dad's beneficiary, was all up my ass to do something about the situation. My first response to her was "Where in the fuck is my dad's old lady? After all these years, why is she taking a step back from assuming responsibility of his care taking right now?!" Clearly my aunt was on his girlfriend's team. Her response to me was "They were never married and if that's what she wants to do, then that is her business. " No doubt She and I didn't see eye to eye on this. So much for trust and loyalty.

Now please keep in mind that I had not had my dad in my life since I was twelve or thirteen years old. I mean he was full blown out of the picture with another woman RAISING HER KIDS AND GRAND KIDS. These years of no dad in the picture really killed me inside because I just wanted to be loved and have someone in my corner that I could talk to and share my life experiences with.

Now, he was in need of hospice care because he could no longer help himself. He could not feed himself. He couldn't even wipe his own ass! So, what did I do?! What would you do?!

I sucked it up, swallowed my pride and did what any man whose intent in life was to do the right thing. I immediately made some phone calls, and got him in a hospice care right next to my house in Newport Beach.

I would go see him every day after a ten plus hour workday in Brea.

I would drive straight to the hospice location to feed him and make sure that he had water every day.

My dad's condition started to wear me down a bit. I was really getting tired of seeing him suffer. I wanted it to end because I knew that he would not be able to fight his way out of this one. I started going home right after work to pick up JD and I was trying to stay positive. I would talk to my dad even though he was never awake, hoping that maybe he would wake up to see JD. The last time that I stood before him, I began to tell him that there was something very valuable that he and my mother had given me as a child. They had taught me how to pray. When I was just a little boy, I used to lie in bed with my mom and dad every night and say the Lord's Prayer. Standing there, I told my dad that he didn't have to fight anymore. I began to pray, "Our Father, who art in heaven..." and instantaneously my mind shot back to 1983. I could see myself praying with my parents as a child. The memory was clear as if it had happened yesterday. As I finished the prayer, I kissed my dad on the forehead and said goodbye. That night, I left the hospice care with tears in my eyes and a heavy heart. Mentally I was exhausted.

The very next day at about 11:00 a.m., as I was teeing off on hole number six at the Santa Ana River View golf course, I was informed that my dad had passed. My heart was sad for the loss. At the same time, I was happy because he would no longer have to suffer. I had seen him through until the very end. I know that God was testing me, and God was the last person that I wanted to disappoint.

In life you will be tested! It's very critical that you pass the test because I guarantee that if you fail...you will have a make-up test. Some lessons are very painful. This is part of the growth process.

When I think about the funeral, it still hurts.

On the day of my dad's funeral, my daughter Ashley wanted to leave before it even started. I knew exactly why she wanted to leave and I asked her to stay out of respect for me, to just please bear with me. Ashley knew about my past and most definitely did not know her biological grandfather the way his girlfriend and her children of over twenty-five years knew him. Ashley felt betrayed by him, just as I had. It didn't end there...

My aunt had asked me to do the eulogy. Please note that I have absolutely no fear of public speaking. As a matter of fact, (not to brag) but I am an awesome speaker and have taken center stage on several occasions, speaking to crowds from one hundred to ten thousand with ease. Some of us are natural at this while others tremble with fear. Without a doubt, I am one of the brave ones.

Now I never practice for these speaking events. I never write stuff down. I just go for what I know. It comes so naturally. But that day, as I recounted my life with dad, I got to age ten and I realized that I had nothing else left to say. I had no good, solid memories with my dad like the memories that my kids have with me. I had so many bad memories and very, very few good ones. I didn't know

134

this man as a real father just as he didn't know me as a real son.

Clearly our relationship was like two old homies who knew each other from way back then. Every time when we parted ways, it was more like "I'll see you when I see you." "See you later."

As I walked off stage and sat down, I heard all his girlfriend's kids get up there and talk about what a good man he was and how he would take them grocery shopping when they needed food. How he would come over and make the best breakfast meals for them and their kids. I listened to them tell about how my dad would show up and take their sons out for haircuts. I was totally floored by this. I felt like I was melting in my seat; I could not wait for this weekend to come to an end.

MEN AND SOME OF YOU WOMEN, do not ever think that it is okay to abandon your own blood to go and be a part of someone else's. It's not right. It's not okay. In fact, it's absolutely unacceptable. Handle your business like a real man, and no matter what, always finish what you start. My stance is extremely strong on the subject of FAMILY FIRST. There are no excuses for abandoning your responsibilities. Cowards run away when life shows you no mercy. But real men and woman will weather the storm and figure out a way for the best outcome that will benefit EVERYONE.

Chapter 32: Resentment Set In

Now that this chapter of my life had come to a close, I was able to focus on my family and myself. My real focal points were on the kids as JD was getting bigger every day and Cody was still very much focused in his year-round sports activities. Ashley was already living on her own, but like most kids who stay in the local area after moving out, she would come over sometimes for dinner or to do some laundry. It was always nice to see her; I was watching her grow into a young and responsible lady.

In all honesty though, for the next three months I felt very odd about my dad's death. For whatever reason, I still could not let go. I had gone to the cemetery a few times with my son JD. All my dead loved ones are buried in Resurrection Cemetery in Rosemead California: Grandpa Tony, Cousin Danny Ramirez aka MEMO, Tia Corrnie and Uncle Louie, Uncle Danny, etc. My wife's family is buried there as well, including both of her grandparents, her Nina Chata and her Uncle Paco. At every visit I made it a point to deliver flowers to all of our family members and say a nice prayer for them, but I would always save my dad for last. I was still full of emotion. To a certain degree, I was angry with him. Standing there at his mausoleum, I closed my eyes and remembered the day of his funeral, his girlfriend's daughter asking me, "Why did we never meet you before all of this took place?" "How come all of these years have gone by and we never knew you?" she asked, as they were closing my dad's ashes at the mausoleum. That day with a heart full of hurt, a ton of anger, and every other uncomfortable emotional feeling that you could possibly feel at a time like that, I still managed to stay calm and gently told her, "Only our parents can answer that question."

After that day, I stopped going to the cemetery. I have not been there ever since.

In the meantime, work was still going well for me, though I was starting to change my mind about some things. I requested a transfer out of Brea and was sent to the home office in Costa Mesa, California. The transfer was accepted, and I was now working a little over two miles away from home. I was now the "King" in my own back yard.

After all the shit I had been through in my life and after all of the goals that I achieved, it was now time to set some new ones.

Exactly what it was that I wanted to do, I just could not figure out. I had this really nice office located upstairs, decorated with fancy wall paintings and designer sofas. I had all these cool family pictures, Dodger pictures, golf pictures, and autographed pictures hanging on the walls.

Out of all these photos that were hanging on the wall, one picture really stood out to me: a photo of the hole #3 at Monarch Beach Golf Course.

The day that picture was taken I had had a great time with my best work buddies. It was a wonderful day on the golf course. Nothing could have gone better that day (except for my shot!), but as I sat at my desk with my feet up, just staring at this picture on the wall, I could not help but think to myself that *I AM WASTING MY LIFE HERE.*

You see from a business perspective, I was not growing anymore. I was not learning anymore. The company was changing DRASTICALLY, and I didn't feel like I fit in anymore. I was changing drastically and I believed that there was a new challenge in life waiting for me.

I am ultra-blessed to have been able to start with this company when we had only four stores in California. I had learned so much in these last ten years. The life lessons that were learned in these buildings are worth millions of dollars. On top of that, I am a very well respected Community Representative, and, most important for me as a person, I had become a role model for MANY. There are several people that looked up to me and needed my guidance.

But for me, all of this was just not enough.

I knew in my heart that God did not bring me this far too just have it all end right there. To spend the next twenty-five years trapped in a building was not what I want to do for the rest of my life. I knew that I was special and that my calling in life would be much more than just being a store manager in the natural food industry. I wanted to reach people by the millions. I wanted to inspire the people of the world to be all that they could possibly be and to help others reach their goals and true life potential.

My wheels were turning day and night in attempt to find a new way of life. This was only the start of a brand-new beginning.

My days off work were Thursdays and Sundays. Lucky for me, up until Cody's junior and senior year in high school all his football games took place on Thursdays, so I was able to make it to every game. On some days during the week, I would head straight to the practice field to watch Cody do his thing. After all this was my passion. Part of reaping what I had sown was seeing my kid participate in all the things that we both loved. These were the things that had I taught him.

I now sit on the side lines with my youngest boy, James Daniel. Being a sideline dad is brutal. I was used to being on the field and calling shots, making adjustments, and being side by side with my kid on the battle field. Yes, letting go is very hard for me. My youngest boy JD loves football and wrestling and reminds me daily that he will follow in his big brother Cody's footsteps. He even picked Cody's football number for his baseball jersey this last season. Clearly JD is Cody's biggest fan. (If you check my Instagram page, there are many great photos of these wonderful times. Please enjoy them.)

Big Brothers and Sisters, you need to be careful of what you do as your younger siblings are watching your every move. They aspire to be what you are and will want to do the things that you do. Whether you like it or not, you are the example. Teach them well.

Now I was enjoying every minute of this part of my life, but as time went on I was looking for a new life. I still didn't know exactly what direction to go in, but I knew that change was on the way and I wanted to be ready for it.

A few more years had gone by and, on my thirty-ninth birthday, I really wanted to get the fuck out of the grocery business. I had grown tired of the politics and the same old bull shit expectations. I was really focused on a new beginning.

In 2016, my annual sales budget was designed for me to miss my sales budget by 1.2 million dollars. The company's expectations were way unaligned with what was actually possible to achieve. In ten years, I have never missed a sales budget. Yeah…talk about a set up for failure. Well, in 2016 I ended up beating my EBITDA (Earnings before taxes amortization and depreciation) by 86 thousand dollars for the year!! Yes!! For 365 days, I micro-managed all four corners of my operation and came out on top!! But that was not good enough. Because I still missed sales by 1.2 million AND I beat my bottom line dollars in overall contribution, the powers-that-be denied my 2016 bonus payout. That was when I really knew that I was just a number to them. No matter what great contributions I gave to my beloved company, it was most evident to me that I was no longer valued. For me this was the last draw. This is when I knew in my heart that I would set on a new path of life. I worked so hard, day in and day out to beat my EBITDA and I micro managed every corner of my building and was still denied a bonus. They got their 14 million in sales for the year and my team and I got nothing. This was the event that tipped the scale for me to seek a new life elsewhere. When you deny good hard-working people out of money that they deserve, don't count on the good help sticking around for very much longer. Ironically, two months later in February of 2017 I received a second Store Manager of the Year award. Now keep in mind we were not a small company anymore with a handful of locations. We now had 300 locations nationwide. That day instead of being happy, I felt really insulted. (As my wife sarcastically joked, "So where is your bonus money?") The point is that I had once again proven only that I was only good enough to make millions of dollars for someone else.

I wanted that money for my family and I was determined to get it!! I knew that there was a better way of life and no doubt I would now work day and night to figure this thing out.

Chapter 33: You can't always win. Failing is part of the growth process.

On the week of my thirty-ninth birthday, I took a long weekend off work to celebrate with my close friends and family. Traditionally on this weekend, we would have a great big huge party at my house with about 60 guest for the opening day of the OC Fair. It's a big deal to me as we all gather at my house, have some beers, enjoy good food, and, MOST IMPORTANTLY, spend time with each other. There are some very important individuals from my past that I only get to see in person about once a year. So we always go all out to make sure that the time spent will be most memorable.

I call this party the DUST BOWL because as soon as the sun goes down, we all walk to the OC Fair in one large group. That weekend was a blast.

That weekend, my actual birthday—July 18—fell on a Sunday. My auntie had come to see me that day. She had been trying to get a hold of me for quite some time. I was very badly hung over from the night before, but I agreed to meet with her in my home. She wanted to show me a new product that she was really excited about. I knew she wanted to sell me something, which I was not too happy about, BUT out of respect, I did not want to be a jerk and just say no. You see, after twenty-nine years,

Nordstrom had just laid her off so that they would not have to pay her retirement. This is a very chicken shit corporate move that happens all the time, and I felt bad for her.

On this Sunday my aunt showed up to the house and brought this really buff ex-Marine with her. He was loud and absolutely annoying. I couldn't stand him, but he had a program that he was very excited about and, again, out of respect for my auntie, I just listened to him ramble on about his program.

They were selling life insurance for Transamerica. Transamerica has some deep pockets. I mean, when it comes to money, they are absolutely fuckin' loaded. I told him that I wanted change in my life, but I was not sure what kind of change would be best for my family and me. I told him that I would think about his offer and get back to him at another time.

One week later my vacation was over, and I ended up going back to work. I must admit that it is very depressing to have to go back to a place that you absolutely dread after a wonderful two week stay at home with the family.

So, the ex-Marine immediately began to hunt me down. He wanted me to join his team. The structure of pay that he presented was awesome. I mean we are talking four to five times that amount of money that I was currently

144

making. No doubt this program was going to take some time to build, but for the first time in almost twenty years James Merrifield decided to try something new.

I now had to complete a forty-hour online practice course before I could actually take a state exam to get my license for selling life insurance. This was all new to me, so I started asking my employees who are college students what they did to cram in their studies and balance out work. I have kids that work for me who go to JC Colleges, State Universities, and even big D1 colleges like USC, ASU, Boise State, Virginia Tech etc. I had not studied for anything like this in several years, so there I was at night, lying in bed knocking out 1.5 hours of online courses a night. This was definitely information overload for me as I did not know anything about state laws or federal guidelines to selling life insurance. I was trying hard to find a new rhythm to my life and this was a start.

Hey, if Colonel Sanders could start a new life at the age of sixty, I was very sure that at thirty-nine I could do the same.

After studying close to thirty-five hours with four more hours to complete the course, I asked my wife to take me to a Barnes and Noble book shop so that I could get a book on Excel formulas as well as a book on closing the deal in sales. I knew that I would have to learn a few new tricks to do well in my new business. I was on a mission and I had to keep the momentum flowing in the right direction.

Chapter 34: Robert Kiyosaki's Book Changed My Life Forever

The summer before I met with my auntie and her new mentor, I kept seeing a guy named Robert Kiyosaki (author of *Rich Dad Poor Dad*) on my Instagram news feed. For the record, I do not know him, nor does he pay me to say the things that I am about to say.

That day at Barnes and Noble, I did not go home with a book on Excel, nor did I go home with a book on closing business deals. I went home with Robert Kiyosakis book titled *Rich Dads Retire Young and Retire Rich*. <u>This would be the book that would change my life and point of view forever</u>. The things that he talked about in that book spoke volumes to my heart and, for the first time in a long time, someone else had really grabbed my attention. Someone else really inspired me to work smarter in life. I have never read an entire book from cover to cover in all of my life, until the day I bought Robert Kiyosaki's book.

Failed test 101:

The forty hours of exam study was complete and in mid-September, I was ready to take my exam. On the day of the exam, I was very excited. I was pumped! I woke up and was singing in the shower and talking a bunch of bullshit to myself like I was in a high school locker room getting ready to play in a championship football game. LMAO. I got in the truck and headed down the 405 South towards the city of Lake Forest and the test was on.

Within the first five minutes, I knew that I was going to fail.

As I began to squirm in my seat, my heart began to break. My good energy went to shit, and, in my mind, I just sat in that chair very slowly bleeding to death. Trust me...when you think that you are ready for something big and you end up failing one of two things will happen. You're either used to fucking up and you just accept the loss or you go in ultra-cocky like I did, fail, and then leave heart broken.

Well that's exactly what happened. I failed the exam.

Two thirds of what was on the actual practice exam was not even relevant to what was on my test. The questions that were on that test were not just some bs multiple choice/one worded answers, but more like multiple choice paragraphs that contained a ton of information. Like I said, information that was not on the study guide.

As I began to drive home I was mad as fuck! I immediately called that lame ass hole recruiter and told him the situation! I cussed him out, and after that, we never spoke again. Then I called my wife to tell her that

I just choked. Because I am always a practical joker, she started to laugh at me and kept telling me to stop lying to her. After a few moments of me not laughing with her, she realized that I was telling her the truth. I told her that I needed to cool off, and that I would see her when she returned home from work. I hung up the phone and my anger came right back. As I drove home my blood began to boil. There was some woman on the radio talking about some political bs. I remember yelling at her to stfu as I smacked the power button to off mode. I was pissed.

When I got home, I parked in the garage and then went and sat down on my back patio ALONE. I painfully waited for my wife to come home. I had to face the music. I had to tell the woman of my dreams WHO I HAD NEVER LET DOWN ONCE IN OVER TEN YEARS, that I failed us. I failed us all. I went straight to the refrigerator and grabbed a beer. After a few shots of tequila, depression set in to my heart and I began to cry.

I'm not in to that losing bs. I felt like I did enough losing in my childhood. I was an adult now and I wasn't supposed to be failing anymore.

My conscience kicked in immediately and began to correct me. Really my conscience is that one thing that truly corrects me and lets me know what I need to work on or what it is that my focal points need to be concerned about.

At all low points in my life my conscience has always saved me from drowning in my sorrow. It always helps me see the good in every bad situation. When your conscience speaks to you, it is very critical that you listen with all your heart and you will learn something new every time something like this happens.

You see win or lose, there was a big lesson that I needed to learn. That lesson was that for twenty years I had been devoted to working my way up to the top in the grocery business. I didn't lose that day of the exam. I won. I won because over the last twenty years I had not attempted to do something new. Something outside of the box. Even though I did not pass the exam, I still attempted to go someplace that I had never been before. You see, lots of times we get so caught up with having tunnel vision as we race towards what we believe is the right path of life. I am so very grateful for my life experiences, BUT I know in my heart that life had something much better for me and I was determined to find it! I was determined to live the life of my dreams!! I was determined to go someplace that no one, not even me, would have ever dreamt possible. This was my first real lesson about failure on my new journey. YOUR GONNA FAIL! YOUR GONNA FUCK UP! THIS IS PART OF THE LEARNING PROCESS! If you are going to be successful, failure is part of the package. You MUST accept EVERYTHING that comes with success. I didn't make it as far as I had in the grocery business overnight, so surely, I would need to learn to be patient with myself during my new career adventure.

Game On!!

From this point on I was reading Robert Kiyosakis book day and night! I was highlighting paragraphs! I was underlining key phrases, quotes, and sentences! I even typed up all the key points and began to email these notes to my kids and my closest friends. I am determined to follow in the footsteps of Robert Kiyosaki as I believe that I would one day find financial freedom and be able to live the life of my dreams just like he had!!

At this point I was very excited about what I learned from the book and was now looking everywhere for clues as to what I could do to push forward to my new goals. I was telling my closest friends about it. Life for James Merrifield was being reborn, only this time I was much more mature and much more willing to do things that I had never done before, go to places where I had never been. In his book, Kiyokakis talks about attending as many free seminars as you can so that you can learn new things, so I started immediately going to business seminars in search of new knowledge.

I was extremely hungry for knowledge and doing research daily to find these seminars and business meetings. On my days off I was no longer racing to the golf course. I was now driving to where ever I had to go to be a part of these seminars. Success was on my mind and this was all that I could think about. I attended about one seminar a week in search of new knowledge and a new life. I was determined to find financial freedom and live the life that I had always wanted to live.

Very Important Information:

For those of you who are looking for something more in life and are just waiting for something to fall from the sky and jump right in to your life...It aint gonna happen. IF YOU WANT TO LEARN SOMETHING NEW YOU ARE GOING TO HAVE TO READ EVERY SINGLE DAY!! This is the only way to take your life in to a different direction. Also there are several different motivational speakers on youtube that you can begin to grow from and learn new things, ideas, and overall success stories.

If you want a new life-you must be willing to do new things. Otherwise you will continue to get the same results doing the same old things. It's your choice.

Chapter 35: Be Careful Who You Trust and Protect Your Money

On one Thursday I went to a real estate seminar in Long Beach California with my wife. It was being taught by someone who claimed to be the number one house flipper in the business, worth about half a billion dollars. Robert Kiyosaki had made a fortune in real estate deals, so I wanted to learn more about this real estate buzz and immediately jumped into the arena of real estate investing with both feet.

I was in for one of the biggest learning lessons of my life.

Between 2016 and 2017, I spent eighty-five thousand dollars to learn how to fix and flip real estate. My wife and I took a three-day, out-of-state bus tour, which we paid 42,500 dollars to be a part of. We completed a three-day Master Mentorship program for almost thirty thousand dollars. We did another three=day out-of-state Cash Flow Course, as well as a three-day out-of-state Asset Protection Course. We even did a two-day Tax Lien seminar that we paid an additional ten thousand for. We opened our own LLC and S Corp so that we could be in the business of fixing and flipping real estate. Like I said, we flew out of state on several occasions to attend seminars and meetings. This was one of the biggest learning lessons of my new venture. What was made out to be so simple was extremely difficult. Not only did I still work my normal ten hour a day job at the grocery store, but I also had to respond and deal with my realtors at all times of the day, check out properties from LA to SD at any time of the day or night. We were making multiple offers a week that were not getting accepted. We were working with hard money lenders who are the absolute sharks of this business and were also looking for private money lenders to support whatever left over funds were needed to close the deal. I worked on this tirelessly in 2017. I was laser focused on success and would not be denied the privilege of someday having financial freedom.

However, I noticed that in other states, the most successful people in the house flipping network were just killing it! There is a big difference in paying sixty to 150 thousand for a fix to flip in the Mid-West or in the Southeast parts of the U.S. versus paying three hundred thousand to over one million for a home in California. We're talking big bucks to flip real estate in California. Big bucks that an unexperienced house flipper like me did not have and I didn't know anyone with deep pockets that would be willing to take a chance on me.

We worked tirelessly for all of 2017 to make our dreams become our new reality. We made about three house offers a day for almost all of 2017 and did not get one offer accepted. We were always getting out bid or the profit margins were not in our favor. After an entire year of grinding it out with the fix and flip game, I decided to call it quits as plan B was now my focus.

Once again, I had failed and this time it was a very, VERY EXPENSIVE failure.

My point is that before getting yourself eighty-five thousand dollars in debt, you really need to do your homework and be extra cautious with trusting anyone when it comes to money. There are many wolves dressed in sheep's clothing and you will find out the hard way if you are not careful. To a certain degree I do feel like I was scammed as several others in this network feel the same way. On the flip side, I really did learn a lot about the real estate investing game. As a matter of fact after I execute plan B, I do plan on going back to plan A but with a much better game plan.

I learned that what was made out to be a full piece of cake was barely a crumb, so be cautious of what you do with your hard-earned money. Do your due diligence and most important make sure that you take intelligent risk.

I could make up every excuse in the world for my failures, but I do accept full accountability for my own actions. Ultimately, it is my job to make myself a success. This responsibility belongs to me and no one else. I know that my FAITH will carry me to my true life calling, and it will be right there that I will find my biggest success.

So, I put the house flipping game aside. My dream of becoming a real estate investor was not gone forever, but plan B was necessary because I was getting burned out and wasn't getting the desired results that I was seeking.

Robert Kiyosaki speaks in his books about going where the investments of the <u>future</u> would be. For me that was a no brainer as technology is the wave of the future and just keeps getting better and better. <u>I had to put my time and energy in focusing on where the world will be going vs where it stands right</u> <u>now.</u> I do not want to miss the next big window of opportunity. When I can afford to fully fund my own real estate deals, I will return to that arena. For now, I continued to focus on self-education in the area of finance and technology.

I make it a point DAILY to learn from the greats such as Grant Cardone, Jim Rohn, Napoleon Hill, Tony Robins, Earl Nightingale, Zig Ziglar, Dan Pena, Tai Lopez, Les Brown, Warren Buffet, Gary Vaynerchuk etc. While driving to work, I listened to a different speaker EVERY DAY. All the things that radio disc jockeys talk about are pure bs and keep small minded people very small. The bottom is way too crowded, and, in a few years, I intend on joining the 5% club.

If you want something different for your life, you will have to be willing to do things that you have never done before. You will have to be willing to change the direction of your sails. The wind is always blowing, but make no mistake, the direction of your sails will, in fact, dictate exactly where you will end up in life. If you are not happy with your current life, I strongly suggest that you adjust the sails.

Finish what you started right? Right!

As my life was changing (and I was gearing up for more changes), my oldest son Cody was getting ready to graduate from high school. He was already enlisted in the US Army because this is what he said he was going to do since he was a freshman in high school. Cody played football more than half of his life and was very good at it. We had always talked about him playing college ball at USC, but as he got older, he developed his own vision as far as what it was that he wanted to do with his life. As parents, we can do our absolute best to influence our children to make WHAT WE BELIEVE are the best choices. However, just remember that their journey belongs to them and OUR JOB is to SUPPORT them no matter what. Our job is to LOVE and GUIDE to the very best of our ability. The rest is on them.

The day of Cody's graduation came, and we were all very excited, but no one showed more excitement than

Cody. The boy had an incredible amount of energy and enthusiasm that filled that entire football stadium. If you couldn't tell by now, I'm a very proud dad! Watching Cody strut up and down the side lines was most memorable. He was so proud of himself and was very anxious to venture off on a new journey with the U.S. Army.

One of my proudest moments was watching Cody run off the field immediately after the graduation ceremony was over and hop over the fence where the track and field are located. With love in his eyes, and a radiant energy full of joy and happiness he sprinted up to the top of the bleachers where our family was sitting and ran straight to his dad for a big hug.

Mission accomplished!

These are the life moments that I live for. These are the moments that made all my hard work and struggles well worth the fight and I am glad that I never gave up. Me and Cody have been a single unit father and son duo that have stuck together like super glue. I am truly blessed as God clearly gave me one of the absolute best gifts that a father could have. He gave me Cody.

Cody had always asked me since he was just a little boy if I was proud of him. He would ask this question after every football game, after every wrestling match, after every A+ that he received on a math test etc. Every time he made the tackle on the field or won a wrestling match, his first reaction was to look in the stands to find me so that he would receive my show of approval or the look of "well done son".

My response to Cody was always the same and never changed.

I told him that I was proud since the day he was born. I was proud since the day I laid eyes on him and held him in my arms. My little buddy would very soon be leaving me and going away to boot camp in Georgia. At this point I laid low for the next few weeks to decompress from the ass whooping's of 2017 until Cody went to boot camp. I needed to recalibrate my mind and take a breather as my plan was to go full speed again right after Cody left for Georgia.

Through all of this in the back of mind I knew that I was going to attack my business with full force as I was not satisfied with the results that I got in 2017. But if you truly knew anything about James Merrifield, you would know that I will not stop until I get what I want. I am not afraid of change or making adjustments. In fact, I can and will adjust all the way up the ladder of success. I know what hard work looks like, I know what it feels like, and I know what it smells like! I will not be denied! I won't stop until I win! After all, self-made billionaire Jack Ma didn't make any money for the first three years in his business. He was always the black sheep when he applied for a job or when he attempted to attend certain schools. He was the king of being denied! Today he is worth over forty billion dollars. His message today remains the same as he expresses that for many years he just could not catch a break and that no one else believed in him but HIMSELF.

How's that for persistency? How is that for having FAITH and BELIEVING in YOURSELF??

New York Rapper Jay-Z also said it best. When asked what was his biggest secret that lead to his footprint being cemented as one of the wealthiest rappers of all time, his answer was a simple as it gets. He stated that "he never gave up." Ultimately persistency is the key to getting what you want in life. Stay persistent. Stay consistent with your efforts, and don't give up! Don't stay down when you get knocked down! No matter how hard it hurts get up off of your back and keep on going! Life was not designed to be a piece of cake! We have to Defy The Odds daily if we are truly going to live a prosperous life!

I turned forty this summer. We did our big OC Fair house party, and we celebrated my birthday. One month later I was dropping off Cody at the recruiter's office where they would be taking my boy to the LAX airport to venture off on a new journey.

Depression really set in that week, and I was sad all the way up to the day that Cody left for Georgia. That Sunday morning, I had a very good feeling of relief and hope. God wasn't letting me do this alone. He and I are one of the winning-est teams in the game of life. I said my prayer. God delivered. End of story.

Cody had never been so far away from me and now I was at a point where I finally had to let go. Letting go of the things that you love most is extremely difficult. I do not believe that there is a way to prep for separation, especially when you have dedicated all your LOVE and ENERGY to the GOOD of a GREATER LIFE cause. However, it must be done as part of life's ultimate purpose.

The ride home was very quiet. My wife was in tears and I was a little numb. JD was very quiet as well, and that night, through the silence of a calm Sunday night, we heard every creek in the house settling. Once again, my life was changing.

Immediately following Cody's departure, I was still doing everything that I could to motivate myself. I donated all his bed room furniture to one of my employees and I turned his room into an office as I was determined to make my home my new work place. I had spent the last year listening to motivational speakers DAILY! I was on a CONSTANT MISSION to

REPROGRAM my brain to thinking in the ways of the MOST successful people. They all had different messages, but one thing that they had in common was that they were all very successful men. EVERY DAY on the way to work, I would listen to a new motivational speaker. I also did this on the way home from work. I was so pumped that I started my own You Tube channel and began giving health tips for people with type 2 diabetes. I began to exercise, talking on camera, and posting these videos online for all to see. In attempt to build an audience, I did several short motivational videos with emphasis on being positive and being your very best. I also did a twenty-five-minute interview sharing with the world exactly who James Merrifield was and what he was all about. I then began filming more videos on being positive and giving back to your community. I had always known what my true calling was and now I fully embraced it.

I paid one thousand dollars to join Tai Lopez's Social Media Marketing Agency Training. The payoff was enormous and I not only learned how to advertise, market, and set up an online business. But I also tapped in to a major network of multi-millionaires who have one thing in common.... Making money.

Clearly the wave of the future is where it's at. That old 9-5 day job will soon be a thing of the past and those who plan to not only survive but remain in positions of leadership, will surely have to either learn or be left behind. The world is changing at a rapid pace. Those who choose to ignore the curve will find out the hard way.

I was so passionate about having a powerful screen presence and learning to be a greater motivational speaker, that I went out and got myself a speaker trainer. He goes by the name of Andy Audate of Audate Enterprises. Andy just happened to be mentored by Keynote Motivational Speaker Les Brown and President of The Les Brown Speaker Institute Eric Stoller. This was a great opportunity for me as my network continues to expand in several different areas of the arena.

My true calling was to be a difference maker and to help others. It took me a little while to truly discover that true calling but once I did, I knew that all I wanted to do was help other people. I wanted to help those individuals who lived a tough life and traveled down the long and turbulent road. Some of these people at one time in their life or another didn't have a choice but to go through some hard times just like I did. But I'm so happy that I am able to relate and coach people up to where they will not only believe in themselves, but so that they can believe in their hopes and dreams and just know that anything in life is possible.

I was called to help others in a way that I could inspire and encourage them to reach their true calling and life potential. One of my mentors Vice President Glade Campbell gave me the nick name THE COACH and that is exactly what I am. I'm very proud of it. Some of the parents of the kids that I worked with in the Pop Warner and Junior All-American football days gave me the title of THE COACH, as well. <u>I coach people both on and off the field of life.</u> I helped people see the bright side of every negative situation and turn it in to a positive. I shared my own life experiences with others to get the best out of them because I knew that this would not only benefit them, but also those who were in their direct surroundings. For many years, I have fostered an environment of love for all the employees that I supervised, for all the kids that I coached, and for all my closest friends and relatives. They knew that they could approach me or call me anytime of the day and I would be there to listen to them and provide the best honest feedback for their personal growth. My main intent was that I was going to make you into a better person whether you liked it or not and I'm forever committed to that.

Of course, I am not perfect, and, yes, I do make mistakes. In fact, I've made several mistakes in my lifetime. But in all fairness to myself and to anyone that I have come in contact with, I can honestly say that I have dedicated my life to serving others. I have dedicated my life to my family and to my community. I've done more right in this world than I have done wrong and that's a fact.

No matter how many times I failed throughout the years, I am still and will always be a champion.

From being a kid who spent the night in school yards, exposed to extreme domestic violence, gang violence, drug and alcohol abuse, I created a great life for my family and me. I built a legacy for my family that will forever be cemented in our family name for all eternity.

****

It is an honor to share my story with you. I did this to show you that no matter what you have been through in your life, there is light at the end of the tunnel. If you will just pick up your feet and stop dragging your heels, you will get to the light at the end of the tunnel and you, too, will be able to feel the joy of self-accomplishment. Trust me when I say that there is no better feeling in the world. You can and will be successful. All you have to do is believe. Believe in yourself. Believe that you were born to win. Believe that no matter what you are going through, you are going to make it. EVERYTHING BEGINS WITH A BELIEF. Make sure that your belief is positive and of good will and, in turn, everything that you could have ever imagined possible will become reality. FAITH is the added ingredient in BELIEF that will make your DREAMS come true.

Last, but not least, is DESIRE.

Desire is what comes from within your heart and keeps FAITH alive to the point of accomplishment. And when that desire turns in to burning desire that is when history is made. That is when great accomplishments are achieved. That is when you too will be able to cement your footprint in history as one of the greats to walk this earth.

I hope that you enjoyed reading this book. Please make it a focal point in your life to get out there and be the best example for others that you can possibly be.

Learn something new every day.

Be the best role model you can be for your family and friends.

And always remember that someone has to lead the pack. Lead well and always do your absolute very best.

Most importantly, love with all of your heart. Your mind is your survival kit, but your heart is what will take you far beyond ANYTHING that you could ever believe would be possible. The heart will always help you to do the right things in life. The HEART is the muscle that powers the SOUL.

Thank You.

Love Always,

James Merrifield

Final Words:
Things That I Have Learned in Life

I'd like to share my wisdom with you. I hope that you will take something from this and apply it to your own daily routines. Add some value to your life. We can only get better, right?

"Unwavering Courage"

This is a term Napoleon Hill uses in his book *Think and Grow Rich.* I love the word "unwavering" as my definition for this word means THERE WILL BE ABSOLUTELY NO BITCHING OUT! There will be no second guessing yourself! You made the choice to take a stand! You made the choice to carry out the plan and now there is no turning back from that decision! Nothing will stop you from success! You will stand up at the gates of success and pound on them until they open up for you! You will own the kingdom of your own glory because you believed in your dreams and you believed in yourself! I speak so passionately about courage because I believe it is step #1 in making a life changing decision. It's the first thing that one must decide within himself before attempting to make the changes for a better life, and maybe even a better world.

Faith

I would have never made it to this point in my life if I did not have my Faith. Faith is intangible. Faith is something that you either have or you don't. It is my belief that in life you must believe in something that is much bigger than yourself. There is no one with whom I have shared my deepest and darkest hours other that Jesus Christ. You may believe in some other God, spirit, person, or thing that keeps you going, and I am not judging you. The point that I am making is that you MUST believe in something bigger that yourself and you MUST have FAITH to carry on in this life. As the majority of all my life's obstacles were extremely challenging, I knew that my FAITH in myself, as well as my faith in God, would pull me through. And it did. Faith backed by BURNING DESIRE is the method to my madness. When I wanted something badly enough, my FAITH mixed with my BURNING DESIRE is what took me to it.

Persistence

Your persistence in achieving a goal will take you there. You will fail, and you will not always get your desired results, but you must stay persistent in your efforts. This is what will allow you to fully reach your destination. With no persistence comes no great reward.

Consistency of Effort

Many people have tried, and many people have failed. You MUST ask yourself the question: *Have I been CONSISTENT?* There are no days off! There is no easy way to the road of success! You either want it or you don't! You will be frustrated and you will become discouraged, but the question still remains....Were you CONSISTENT with your efforts???!!! Stay CONSISTENT in anything that you do which relates to personal success and just know that it never hurts to add some additional effort.

Develop Your Discipline

Discipline is the key to my personal success. This took me several years to develop, but I knew in my heart that the only way to success was to stay disciplined in all areas of my life. Discipline is not like a light switch. You cannot just turn it on and off as you wish. If your desire is to be successful in any way, you have got to be able to develop a discipline strong enough to withstand your desires.

The power of setbacks

After life knocks you down, you MUST get back up on your feet and fight again. Setbacks are intangible. No one ever sees them coming. Some individuals NEVER recover from the setbacks of life. To me a setback is life asking you, "How bad do you really want this?" and at this point you must make a big decision. You can either stay down, or you can get up. The choice is yours. I have had several setbacks in my life, but through perseverance, I was able to turn tragedy into triumph. I stayed consistent in all my efforts to be better than I was at the time of setback. Know that after a setback, OPPORTUNITY will present itself again and the best thing that you can do is BE READY for the RESPOSIBILITY when it returns. It will return.

Execution and Accountability

Execution to me means getting it done, no matter what! This is one of my biggest strengths! I get it done! I work with whomever I need to get the job done! ACCOUNTABILITY is a huge factor. I have found that the world has abandoned this ESSENTIAL LIFE TRAIT. The most successful men and women have mastered accountability. They take full blame for their OWN ACTIONS. If things do not work to their plan, rather than place blame on others, they hold THEMSELVES ACCOUNTABLE. This is the right thing to do. Staying honest with yourself is a wonderful quality and must be a daily practice.

Heart and Soul

Put your heart and soul in to everything that you do. Your heart will take you to places that you never thought that you would be able to see. Think of your life's greatest accomplishments. No matter what just came to your mind, I guarantee that your heart is what took you there. Your heart is what made your dream or achievement come true. The heart will carry you in life, but you MUST make it a priority to take care of your heart.

Coaches and Mentors

We all need a coach and a mentor. This is essential to one's success. PLEASE REMEMBER that success comes in MANY DIFFERENT FORMS and not just money or material things. The coaches of the world will make you better whether you like it or not. There will be times when they will make you feel uncomfortable and that is good. This is part of the process. Coaches at times must break you down to build you back up. It is their job to create and groom a better you. Mentors are those who will guide you in the realm of success. They will be those individuals who will lead by example and will not allow you for one minute to believe that your shortcomings are acceptable. These people will be found in your schools, your work places, and your networks. If you cannot find a mentor, you can always YouTube a mentor as there are SEVERAL individuals on line who are outstanding in the areas of personal development.

Love

I believe that LOVE is most ESSENTIAL in life. This is the best intangible feeling that carries one through life. To a certain degree, one can see it through expression, but the feeling is medicine to the soul. The medicine needed for an eternity. While I believe in this great gift of LOVE, I want to stress that you must LOVE yourself. Over the last twenty years I worked tirelessly in life to not allow history to repeat itself. I gave my heart and soul to working hard for my children and wife, my community, my workplace. <u>I did not focus on loving myself</u>. This is now a major focal point in my life, as I believe that the more you LOVE YOURSELF the more you will be able to love EVERYTHING else in this world. Love that flourishes from within has no end. There are no limits to what the miracle of love can do. With no love in the heart, your soul is doomed. Love will open doors that you never knew existed.

An Attitude of Gratitude

Daily, upon wakening, I give thanks to my Creator. I give thanks for the roof over my head, the blanket I am wrapped up in, the clothes on my body, the shoes on my feet, the food on the table, the reliable transportation that gets us to and from, and so on. I even pray in the shower. When you begin your day with an attitude of gratitude, you are not allowing any negative thoughts to transpire into your day. These thoughts of negativity (if allowed in) will ruin your day and will even ruin your life. If perception is reality, you must learn to perceive in a positive manner.

Content of Environment

You must be extra cautious with what you let into your mind!! In the car on the way to work or even just going to the grocery store, I choose to listen to a new motivational speaker so that I can increase my overall knowledge of being a better human being. Radio DJs flood the airwaves with things of little or no value at all, so I choose to listen to those individuals with PROVEN track records of success. These individuals are the ones who I am trying to be like, even to a certain degree mirror, but overall, I do this to increase my wisdom so that I may be of greater influence for those whom I may encounter.

Trust and Loyalty

For ONLY the RIGHT REASONS, it is very critical that you remain loyal to those who you are closest to. Trust must be established immediately and may take some time to build. But once the cycle is complete YOU MUST NEVER betray those you have your back!! You have all heard the saying that trust takes a lifetime to build and only one minute to be broken FOREVER. Staying honest with others is the only way to go. Your

INTEGRITY will be on display for others to view at all times. It only takes one shady move to lose the respect of your entire following.

The Inner Circle

I gave everything that I had to my inner circle. My wife and my children complete this circle. Though my two oldest children are gone off to find their own way, they are strong-minded and strong-willed because that is what I taught them. Whatever you sacrifice your life for, be sure that it is for the most noble cause. KEEP THE CIRCLE TIGHT AND KEEP IT CLOSED. As my wife and I are now alone with our youngest son. Our time and energy are now focused on the three of us. We are focused on grooming a five-year-old boy to excellence and we are focused on loving one another to the best of our abilities. Distractions will arise, but it is most critical to remember that these distractions DO NOT belong to you nor are they your DIRECT PROBLEMS. Therefore, you must choose to keep the gates of your inner circle shut; do not allow anyone or anything to penetrate the walls of your castle. Third party problems destroy peace and ruin intimacy. It is YOUR JOB to protect your family.

Take the time to listen to others

People just want to be heard. They don't always want a solution. If you can give them one, they will be grateful for it, but ultimately, they just want someone to listen. Listening shows that you care and always remember that you just might learn something from being a good listener.

Negativity on Social Media

Anything that does not help you grow must go!! Delete all individuals who are constantly being downers and who have no problem with sharing every negative episode of their lives. Do not allow perfect strangers to dictate your overall mental well-being. You have the responsibility to protect the gates of your mind. Any individual who is TOXIC to your overall well-being MUST NOT have a place in YOU LIFE.

Protect your wallet

There are several wolves in sheep's clothing on line. Do your DUE DILLIGENCE before spending big dollar amounts with these so-called online gurus. Google them for references, ask those on line who are in their networks to prove their earnings. And remember majority rules when asking for references. That means if everyone is saying don't do it, **don't do it**. These individuals have made millions off preying on the ambitious. The ambitious must do their homework before making big money spending decisions.

Reflection

When you reflect on your life, it is very important to reflect on the good. I've had many heartbreaks and upsets in my life. If you choose to reflect on the negatives, then your mind will be clouded by negativity. This will tear you down from time to time and will make it very difficult for you to be built back up. You have a choice. I speak from experience when I say that you need to focus on keeping your reflections and your thoughts a positive as you can possibly be. Choose well.

Help Others In Need

Zig Ziglar told us through his teachings that if you help enough other people get what they want, this will bring you closer to getting what you want. Helping other is the right thing to do. A helpful mindset is a great way to stay in constant interaction and engagement with others. You will get to learn more about others by staying close to them and their needs. This is a great way to stay in what is called "down to earth" so that you don't forget that we are all human and that we all have needs.

Jim Rohn said "for things to change, you have to change. For things to get better, you have to get better, For things to improve, you have to improve." You see, everything begins and ends with you. You have the freedom to choose whatever your heart so desires to do. If change is what you desire you have to stay committed to working on a new you day in and day out! There is no getting around or away from the reality of desired self-improvement. You will either put the time and energy in to a better you. Or on the other hand, you will remain the same until you develop the courage to commit to change.

Les Brown has many wonderful quotes. But his truest quote to me is that if you want something bad enough in your life "You gotta be hungry!" I believe that is what it all comes down to. Yes, if you want it bad enough, well then you gotta be hungry.

A lot of motivational speakers will talk about FEAR being the major contributor of people not reaching their true potential. But in this day in age I will fully disagree with that belief. It is my personal belief that there are many brave souls wondering on this earth who are in desperate need of a mentor. One person can fully change the life of another. Not only will they change the life of another but they can change the course of an entire family bloodline. An entire culture can be redirected to greatness due to the help of one individual who is willing to make a difference in someone else's life.

Think about it.

That is why it is so important for ALL OF US to help ONE ANOTHER.

Defying The Odds.

Stay Defiant In Your Search For Success.

CPSIA information can be obtained
at www.ICGtesting.com
Printed in the USA
FSHW011504040619
58724FS